Angry Schnauzer Prese

ENGLISH I

THiS BOOK BELONGS TO:

_____

ACING the STAAR, ENGLISH I was made for you, the student, to improve your success on the end of year examination. Your education is our **#1 Goal** and this workbook is packed with fun, helpful knowledge to put you on the path to success!

We wish you the best with your Academic Achievements!

The Angry Schnauzer, Ltd. is a small puppy and owner run business dedicated to bringing you fun and creative educational books and merchandise for you to enjoy. Please keep us in mind and check back often - New items added frequently.

Thank you for your purchase!

Have questions?	Want to know more?
Let us know at:	Visit us at:
Support@TheAngrySchnauzer.com	*www.TheAngrySchnauzer.com*

About the Workbook:

Congratulations on your purchase!

Acing the STAAR, English I was developed from the foundation up with Texas board-certified teachers, using the latest Texas Essential Knowledge and Skills (TEKS) to support and enhance classroom learning and the State of Texas Assessments of Academic Readiness (STAAR) test success.

The primary goal of this workbook is to improve student success on the end of year STAAR test. To accomplish this goal, every major area of English I instruction, divided by topic area, is included.

Within each topic area, for example, Fiction, Poetry, Drama, etc., students will find a **Topic Introduction**, **Defined Core Vocabulary** list, a fun **Painless Practice** worksheet, representative STAAR test **Reading Passages**, **Questions** and an **Expository Essay** practice, as well as **Testing Tips** and a thoughtful **Mindful Moment** brain break exercise.

In addition to helping students find success on the STAAR, one of the primary goals in the development of *Acing the STAAR, English I* was to support classroom learning in an engaging way that amplifies and enhances direct instruction through scaffolding. Because the workbook follows the Texas English I Year at a Glace (YAG) curriculum, it can easily be inserted to aid with teaching and provide a secondary reinforcement and practice opportunity for students.

Students Using the Workbook for STAAR Test Preparation:

This workbook will augment what you've learned over the course of (or during) the school year. It can be completed throughout the year to reinforce your learning, or prior to the STAAR test as a quick refresher that will prepare you with questions and essays that are similar to ones you will face on the real exam. Your education is our **#1 Goal** and we believe this workbook will aid you along on your personal road to success!

Although you can work through the book in any order you'd like, within each major topic area, we highly suggest you follow the workbook's course of instruction. In addition, don't cheat yourself and skip the **Painless Practice** and **Testing Tips** sections. These contain invaluable information and hints that will improve your test score.

Whether you follow the workbook cover-to-cover, or jump around and cover topics as desired, we are confident ***Acing the STAAR, English I*** will provide a wealth of knowledge that can help reduce test anxiety, increase test knowledge and enhance your ability to Ace the STAAR!

Teachers Using the Workbook to Support Instruction:

This workbook was created to follow the TEKS Resource System English I YAG and is written in the following order: **Writing: Editing and Revision** (Foundations of Reading and Writing); **Fiction, Poetry, Drama** (Literary Texts); **Informational Texts** (Informative Texts); **Argumentative Texts** (Argumentative Texts); **Connections across Genres** (Finding Connections).

Although the workbook was created to follow the English I YAG recommended curriculum, it may be used in any major topic order desired.

For example, the Informational Text section could be accomplished ahead of the Fiction (or any other) section if desired.

This allows the workbook to support individual instruction differences while still providing a scaffolding option to give students additional learning and practice opportunities.

In addition, we tagged each question within the workbook with the TEKS learning objective we applied to the particular question. This was done strictly for you as a way to convey the TEKS applied throughout the sections. These are found in three places, on the line below the questions tied to reading passages, in the same location in the answer key and on a TEKS applied by section summary page.

For You: The end of this book contains a few teacher resources that support your use of this workbook in your instruction, including the TEKS summary, a vocabulary summary and grading sheets. These support resources were made with the desire to help you in any way possible to increase your student's success.

Helpful Hint: We have provided the answers (with detailed explanations) for the review questions at the back of the book. Although optional and strictly at your discretion, we kindly suggest removing these pages prior to handing out the workbooks to your students.

Finally, we hope you enjoy using these workbooks to augment your teaching. We believe this book can give you another tool to help you construct your own plan of instruction for a successful school year. We wish you the best of luck with your instruction and hope you have a great year!

Editing Characteristics:

You've written your essay; "That's great!" But you're not done yet. An essential step to any writing process is Editing. When you edit your writing, you're looking for mistakes such as spelling errors, misplaced punctuation, capitalization, word tense, etc. No matter how great the essay content, these simple mistakes can be a deal breaker

Editing is the act of correcting errors in grammar, punctuation, spelling and structure at the sentence level.

Steps in the Editing process:

- Read each sentence individually to check for errors (**Think:** Going over it with a fine-tooth comb)
- Use a dictionary to verify the spelling and definitions of your word choices
- Ensure none of your sentences are fragments or run-ons (**Think:** Incomplete thoughts, or excessive use of and / or)
- Verb tenses – Ensure verbs agree within a sentence (**Think:** I ate yogurt for breakfast, it is delicious – either change "is" to "was" or "ate" to "eat")
- Noun – pronoun (pronoun antecedent) agreements – Ensure nouns and pronouns within a sentence are paired (**Think:** The dog is huge for their age – the word "their" is incorrect as "The dog" is singular – "their" should be replaced with "its", or the correct masculine or feminine pronoun, "his", or "her")
- Verify your punctuation is correct and effective. Common errors include:
  - Missing commas to separate clauses before coordinating conjunctions (**Think:** F.A.N.B.O.Y.S – For, And, Nor, But, Or, Yet, So)
  - Missing commas after introductory phrases (**Think:** When I woke up, I got dressed.)
  - Missing commas when setting off quotes (**Think:** Maria said, "I love chocolate.")
  - Missing semicolons when combining independent clauses (**Think:** John needed food; he called Uber Eats.)
  - Misplaced apostrophes that change meanings from possession to contraction (**Think:** Its – possessive vs it's – it is)
  - Misplaced apostrophes that change possession (**Think:** "Lions" is two or more lions vs "**lion's**" means something belongs to a single lion vs "**lions'** "means something belongs to two or more lions)
- Capitalization is correct (**Think:** M.I.N.T.S – Months, I, Names, Titles, Starts of Sentences)

Examples of Editing sentences:

(1) Alice is the ninth grades class president because their was no students who run against her. (2) She ran unopposed, she threatened her piers not to run. (3) We we're all to nervous to run because. (4) They compare her to kim jong-un. (5) Next year we will stage a coup elect a new president and prevent this tradgey from happening again so we dont have to do the bow every time she passes us down the hall.

- (1) – Alice is the ninth **grade's** class president because **there were** no students who **ran** against her.
- (2) – She ran unopposed**;** she threatened her **peers** not to run.
- (3) – We **were** all **too** nervous to run because **(fragment – remove the period)**
- (4) – **they** compare her to **Kim Jong-un**.
- (5) – Next year**,** we will stage a coup, elect a new president and prevent this **tragedy** from happening again. **(run on – separate the sentence) This is** so we don't have to do the bow every time she passes us down the hall.

The paragraph rewritten:

Alice is the ninth grade's class president because there were no students who ran against her. She ran unopposed; she threatened her peers not to run. We were all too nervous to run because they compare her to Kim Jong-un. Next year, we will stage a coup, elect a new president and prevent this tragedy from happening again. This is so we don't have to bow every time she passes us down the hall.

- **Conventions** – Standards in the use of written language.

- **Craft / Style** – The tools an author uses to produce uniquely structured writing (**Think:** An author's craft is their personal way of writing.)

- **Publish** – To issue a written work for others to read.

- **Noun** – Person, Place or Thing (**Think:** Bob, school, pencil.)

- **Pronoun** – A word that takes the place and function of a Noun (**Think:** I, she, their, it.)

- **Verb** – Action, State, or Occurrence (**Think:** looked, sit, find, became, happen.)

- **Adverb** – A word that modifies a verb, often by using 'ly' (**Think:** boldly, softly, rapidly.)

- **Adjective** – A word to describe a noun or pronoun (**Think:** happy, yellow, thin.)

- **Punctuation** – Marks in a piece of writing that add clarity to the sentences (**Think:** Commas, periods, semicolons.)

- **Syntax** – The (proper) arrangement of words in a sentence (**Think:** Broke Bob the glass (incorrect) vs Bob broke the glass (correct).)

- **Complete Sentence** – A sentence with, at least, a Subject (usually a noun or pronoun), Verb (an action word) and Object (the thing the subject is acting upon.)

- **Independent Clause** – Contains Subject, Verb and Object to express a complete thought (Independent clauses are complete sentences.)

- **Dependent Clause (Sentence Fragment if used without an Independent Clause)** – Contains a Subject and Verb, but does not express a complete thought.

  - **Noun Clause** – A dependent clause that functions as a noun (**Think:** "I know **that I can pass the exam**." The words, "that I can pass the exam," form the noun clause. **Note:** you can identify noun clauses with a pronoun. If you replace the noun clause above with a pronoun, "I know **it**," the sentence still functions as a complete sentence. This means the words, "that I can pass the exam," are functioning as a noun clause.)

- o **Adjective Clause** – A dependent clause that modifies a noun or pronoun (**Think:** "Students **who are successful** listen to their teachers." The words, "who are successful," form the adjective clause to modify the noun, "Students.")
- o **Adverb Clause** – A dependent clause that modifies another adverb, verb or an adjective to (usually) add conditional information (**Think: "If you drive to school**, you have more freedom." The words, "If you drive to school," form the adverb clause with the condition that you must drive to school to have more freedom.)
- • **Structure** – The way sentences are composed based on the clauses used.
  - o **Simple Sentence** – An independent clause (**Think:** I ran a marathon.)
  - o **Compound Sentence** – Two or more independent clauses (**Think:** I ran a marathon, and I won first place.)
  - o **Complex Sentence** – An independent clause and one or more dependent clauses (**Think:** I ran a marathon and was very tired afterwards.)
  - o **Compound-Complex Sentence** – Two or more independent clauses and one or more dependent clauses (**Think:** I ran a marathon; I won first place and was very tired afterwards.)
- • **Conjunction** – Words used to: Connect dependent clauses or independent clauses; Coordinate words within a clause; or, Connect independent and dependent clauses.
  - o **Coordinating Conjunction** – Connect words, clauses or phrases of equal importance (**Think:** Two dependent or two independent clauses – most commonly: For, And, Nor, But, Or, Yet, So – **Acronym:** FANBOYS.)
  - o **Correlative Conjunction** – Pairs of words that work together to compare two parts of a sentence (**Think:** Both…and, Not only…but also, Either…Or, Neither…Nor, Whether…Or.)

Coordinating Conjunction Express

- **Subordinating Conjunction** – Joins independent clauses with dependent clauses, making the dependent clause less important.
  - **Think:** After, Although, As if, Because, Even though, How, If, Now that, Once, Since, That, Until, When, Where, While, etc.
  - **Note:** Like the dependent clauses they modify, subordinating clauses may be used at the beginning of a sentence or after an independent clause.
  - **Examples:**
    - **After** John went to school, he hurried to class (note the use of the subordinating conjunction at the beginning of the sentence.)
    - John hurried to class, **after** he went to school (note the use of the subordinating conjunction after the independent clause.)
- **Active Voice** – The subject performs the action (**Think:** The student earned the grade.)
- **Passive Voice** – The subject receives the action (**Think:** The grade was earned by the student.)
- **Run-on Sentence** – Occurs when two independent clauses are connected without proper punctuation or coordinating conjunctions.
  - **Comma Splice** – Two independent clauses are joined by only a comma (**Think:** "They went home, they had food." Adding a period, a semicolon, or a comma and any of the many coordinating conjunction choices fixes the issue. **For example:** "They went home, **and** they had food.".)
  - **Fused Sentence** – Two independent clauses are joined without punctuation or coordinating clauses, or excessive conjunctions (**Think:** "They went home they had food," and "They went home and they had food and they were full." The first example could be fixed by adding a period, a semicolon, or a comma and conjunction after the word home, just like with the comma splice. There are many ways to fix the second example, but the simplest would be to add a period at the end of one of the independent clauses and to use a conjunction on the other. **For example:** "They went home. They had food, and they were full.")

- **Subject – Verb – Pronoun Agreement** – Almost always, the parts of a sentence should agree. If the subject is plural, the verb and any pronouns would also be plural. The difference between singular and plural can be quite small, but it makes a huge difference. **Think:**
  - "The boy is sitting in his class." (1 student, 1 class)
  - "The boys are sitting in their class." (2 or more students, 1 class)
  - "The boys are sitting in their classes." (2 or more students, 2 or more classes)

- **Verb Tense Consistency** – All verbs within a sentence are in the same tense - Past, Present or Future (**Think: "She ran** so fast when she **is running** track." In this sentence, "ran" (past tense) is not in agreement with "is running" (present tense). The verb tense should be changed to match the intended tense of the sentence. **For example:** "She ran so fast when she ran track," would place the sentence in past tense.)

- **Noun – Pronoun (Pronoun Antecedent) Agreement** – Pronouns must agree with their Nouns (Antecedent – meaning first used noun) and be either plural or singular. **Think:**
  - (*Incorrect*) – When **a student** (singular) has been studying, **they** (plural)are likely to pass.
  - (Correct) – When **a student** (singular) has been studying, **he** (or she – singular) is likely to pass.   **Or**
  - (Correct) – When **students** (plural) have been studying, **they** (plural) are likely to pass.

PARTS OF SPEECH

It is essential to know what category each word is assigned to in order to use them properly. And learning them isn't as hard as it seems!

PARTS OF SPEECH:

The five major parts of speech with their definitions and examples are below

NOUN

Person, place thing, or idea
Daniel, bike, love

PRONOUN

takes place of a noun
I, he, she, they

ADJECTIVE

describes a noun
blue, cute, loud

VERB

shows an action
live, run, sit

ADVERB

describes a verb
slowly, very, happily

Practice: Mad Libs

Directions: fill in the blanks with any word that fits that part of speech to create your own story!

Yesterday, _____ went to the _____ zoo.
          pronoun   noun

It was a _____ experience filled with
         adjective

_____ _____ and _____.
  adjective   plural noun   plural noun

_____ was there and _____
famous person (noun)   past tense verb

_____. Overall, it was _____,
   adverb   adjective

but _____ began to _____ at the
    noun   verb

_____ enclosure. It was so very
  noun

_____ when the _____.
  adjective   plural noun

started to _____ _____. Once
         verb   famous person (noun)

that happened, I said, "This is one _____
                            adjective

Zoo! I can't wait to _____ it again."
                verb

HOMOPHONES

Homophones are two or more words with the same pronunciation but different spellings and meanings. This leads to lots of misunderstandings and mistakes!

HOMOPHONES:

Don't get confused, we're here to help! Learn the differences between each word.

YOUR
belongs to you
I have your dog

YOU'RE
you are
you're the best

TO
towards / infinitive
to the gym / to dance

TWO
2
I bought two tickets

TOO
also
I want to go, too

THEIR
belongs to them
their cat is cute

THERE
location
I live over there

THEY'RE
they are
they're my neighbors

ITS
belongs to it
its paws are huge

IT'S
it is
it's a great day

AFFECT
verb
his tone affected me

EFFECT
noun
freckles are an effect from the sun

Practice: Tweets

Directions: write a tweet for each group of homophones that includes them all

Expert Tester ✔ @acedSTARRtest   2h

> **You're guaranteed to succeed if you get your head in the game and try your best!**

Expert Tester ✔ @acedSTARRtest   2h

Expert Tester ✔ @acedSTARRtest   2h

Expert Tester ✔ @acedSTARRtest   2h

Expert Tester ✔ @acedSTARRtest   2h

Read the selection, then choose and circle the best answer to each question.

Emilia's teacher asked her to write an expository essay expressing her thoughts on failure. Read her paper and think about any corrections she needs to make. Once you finish reading, answer the questions that follow.

How Failure can Strengthen a Person

By Emilia Anderson

(1) On July 4, 1776, the Second Continental Congress announced their separation from Great Britain with the Declaration of Independence. (2) They were led. (3) By George Washington, the Commander in Chief of the Continental Army. (4) While you may know that he led the country to victory at Yorktown in 1781, did you also know he was a failure? (5) In fact, on another fourth of July, around 20 years earlier, Washington was forced to abandon fort Necessity in a defeat to the French. (6) Defeat in battle can hardly be seen as a positive, but Washington used this defeat to shape and mold the battle strategies he used to overcome the British during the Revolutionary War. (7) By learning from his mistakes and overcoming them, they turned failure and disappointment into victory and joy. (8) Failure is an opportunity for growth because it provides possibilities to learn from our mistakes and develop new responses to overcome them.

(9) Like Washington, we can also use our failures to build future success. (10) The act of failing in and of itself is not a bad thing, it simply adds to our knowledge of what does and does not work. (11) Failing over and over, but continuing to try, builds our character and makes us more aware of what it takes to succeed, moreover, as long as we kept trying, there is still the possibility of succeeding. (12) Every failure puts us one step closer to success and eliminates one more wrong path for us to go down. (13) It is only when we give up that failure truly wins.

(14) Thus, failure should be seen as opportunity. (15) Opportunity to grow. (16) Opportunity to build. (17) Opportunity to become better. (18) If we seize this opportunity, learn from our mistakes, and develop new strategies we will eventually succeed. (19) The road may be difficult, and we may sometimes have to surrender, but waiting on the other side of our failures: is victory. (20) Understanding that a simple failure is not the end, but only the begining, we can take heart, grow stronger and develop in confidence our way forward.

1 What change, if any, needs to be made in sentence 3?

   A Change the sentence to read: **George Washington was the Commander in Chief of the Continental Army**.

   B Change the sentence to read: **By George Washington, who was the Commander in Chief of the Continental Army**.

   C Change the sentence to read: **The Commander in Chief of the Continental Army was George Washington**.

   D Combine sentences 2 and 3 to eliminate sentence fragment

E1.9(D)(i)

2 Which of the following sentences is an example of a run-on sentence?

   F Sentence 20

   G Sentence 11

   H Sentence 6

   J Sentence 4

E1.9(D)(i)

3 Which verb tense is used incorrectly?

   A **Kept** in sentence 11

   B **Led** in sentence 4

   C **Were** in sentence 2

   D **Have** in sentence 19

E1.9(D)(ii)

4 What change, if any, needs to be made in sentence 7?

    F Add a comma after **disappointment**

    G Change *his* to **their**

    H Change *they* to **he**

    J No change is necessary

E1.9(D)(iii)

---

5 What change, if any, should be made to sentence 5?

    A Change *fort* to **Fort**

    B Change *fourth* to **4th**

    C Change *fourth* to **Fourth**

    D No change should be made

E1.9(D)(iv)

---

6 What is the correct way to write sentence 18?

    F If we seize this opportunity, learn from our mistakes, and develop new strategies we will eventually succeed.

    G If we seize this opportunity; learn from our mistakes, and develop new strategies, we will eventually succeed.

    H If we seize this opportunity, learn from our mistakes, and develop new strategies, we will eventually succeed.

    J If we seize this opportunity; learn from our mistakes, and develop new strategies we will eventually succeed.

E1.9(D)(v)

7 What change, if any, should be made in sentence 19?

   A Change the colon after **failures** to a comma

   B Change the colon after **failures** to a semicolon

   C Remove the colon after **failures**

   D No change should be made

E1.9(D)(v)

8 What change, if any, needs to be made in sentence 20?

   F Add a comma after **that**

   G Change *begining* to **beginning**

   H Add a comma after **stronger**

   J No change is necessary

E1.9(D)(vi)

9 Which of the following sentences contains a run-on sentence caused by a comma splice?

   A Sentence 11

   B Sentence 6

   C Sentence 10

   D Sentence 20

E1.9(D)(i)

Read the selection, then choose and circle the best answer to each question.

Viktor's teacher asked him to write an expository essay expressing his dreams about the future. Read his paper and think about any corrections he needs to make. Once you finish reading, answer the questions that follow.

My Best Self: Today, Tomorrow, Forever

By Viktor Machuga

(1) Time and tide wait for no one. (2) This saying, attributed as early as 1225 to saint Mahrer, is a warning as much as it is guidance. (3) Our lives, much like the sand in an hourglass, drips constantly down until the last grain falls into the pile, and it ends. (4) How many grains of sand we have is unknown. (5) What we do with each of those grains was entirely our choice. (6) My dream for the future is to, right now, focus on becoming my best self, live my best life, do my best in everything I try and to be the person I am meant to become.

(7) If we embrace the lesson of the hourglass, time and the tide, we must understand the future is now. (8) It might be to late to start working on dreams for the future tomorrow, because the future has already come. (9) Tomorrow, and the next day, and the next; time is constantly moving forward. (10) With or without us, so we must struggle against quitting or stopping. (11) Since our futures start today, any dream we have for our future must also have action today to make that dream come to fruition. (12) If I am to meet my ultimate goal of becoming the person I am meant to become, I must work always, today, to become that person.

(13) It is not easy to become your best self. (14) It's hard to have the strength to move forward every day, but if you dream of becoming your best self, you must. (15) My dream for the future is to live in the now, by growing daily, constantly fighting against quitting and to work towards becoming who we are supposed to become. (16) I will live in the now today, tomorrow, forever. (17) My best life, my dream life, starts today.

1   What error was made in sentence 10 and how can it be fixed?

   A   Comma Splice – place a semicolon after the word **us**

   B   Sentence Fragment – combine lines 9 and 10 with a comma

   C   Verb Tense Consistency – change **struggle** to **struggled**

   D   Pronoun – Antecedent Agreement – change **we** to **they**

E1.9(D)(i)

2   What is the correct way to write sentence 13 in the active voice?

   F   To become your best self is not easy

   G   Your best self to become is not easy.

   H   Becoming your best self is not easy.

   J   No change – sentence already in active voice

E1.9D(ii)

3   Which of the following words is misspelled?

   A   The word **to** in sentence 8

   B   The word **fruition** in sentence 11

   C   The word **strength** in sentence 14

   D   The word **tomorrow** in sentence 16

E1.9D(vi)

4 What is the best way to write sentence 16?

    F   I will live in the now today, tomorrow; forever.

    G   I will live in the now today: tomorrow, forever.

    H   I will live; in the now today, tomorrow, forever.

    J   I will live in the now: today, tomorrow, forever.

E1.9D(v)

---

5 What change, if any, needs to be made in sentence 2?

    A   Insert a semicolon after Mahrer

    B   Change *is guidance* to **was guidance**

    C   Change *saint* to **Saint**

    D   No change is needed in sentence 2

E1.9(D)(iv)

---

6 What error, if any, was made in sentence 15 and how can it be fixed?

    F   Fused Sentence – place a semicolon after the word **daily**

    G   Pronoun – Antecedent Agreement – change *we are* to **I am**

    H   Comma Splice – Divide 15 into two sentences at the word **now**

    J   Sentence 15 does not contain an error

E1.9(D)(iii)

7 Where should quotations have been applied in the essay?

  A Around sentence 12

  B Around sentence 6

  C Around sentence 17

  D Around sentence 1

E1.9(v)

---

8 What is the correct way to write sentence 5?

  F What we do with each of those grains is entirely our choice.

  G What we do with each of those grains, was entirely our choice.

  H What we do with each of those grains, is entirely our choice.

  J What we do with each of those grains was entirely our choice.

E1.9(D)(ii)

MINDFUL moment

Studies have shown that mindfulness (a calming technique to bring you to the present) decreases stress and increases focus! Coloring is an excellent mindfulness exercise!

THE HIGHER YOU JUMP, THE HIGHER YOU'LL LAND!

WRITING: Revision

ESSAY CLEANING

Revision Characteristics:

So, you've edited your essay and fixed all your mistakes. Awesome work, but you're not done yet! Writing also needs Revision to ensure it flows, stays on topic and maintains coherency. This too is an important step in the writing process. It's the step where the author's voice and word choice are especially important and is the last chance to make your words resonate with the reader.

Revision is the act of rearranging, adding, removing or changing aspects of the writing to improve clarity, flow and organization.

Steps in the Revision process:

- Check for a clear thesis statement that relays the main idea of the text
- Ensure there is a clear organization to the essay with logically developed paragraphs
    - The introduction has a hook, clear transitions and contains the thesis
    - The body paragraph(s) begins with a topic sentence, and includes one or more concrete examples that support the thesis
    - The conclusion sums up the essay, restates the thesis in a new way and leaves the reader with a thought-provoking statement or call to action
- Remove or change sentences that do not support the paragraph's topic sentence or veer from the main idea of the essay
- Confirm transitions between sentences and paragraphs are clear and are not formulaic (**Think:** Saying, "In conclusion" in the conclusion paragraph, is redundant)
- Inspect the entire essay for word choice, fine details and message effectiveness

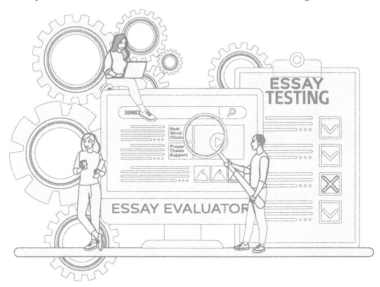

Examples of Revising writing: (This is an Introductory paragraph)

(1) Alice is the ninth grade's class president because there were no students who ran against her. (2) She ran unopposed; she threatened her peers not to run. (3) We were all too nervous to run because they compare her to Kim Jong-un. (4) Next year, we will stage a coup, elect a new president and prevent this tragedy from happening again. (5) This is so we don't have to do the bow every time she passes us down the hall.

- The paragraph needs a hook that grabs the reader.
   o **Add:** before (1) – Our freshman class is in need of a revolution.
- Sentence (2) is awkwardly composed.
   o **Rearrange:** (2) – She threatened her peers not to run, so she could run unopposed.
- Missing transition between sentences (2) and (3).
   o **Add:** transition "Also," to beginning of (3) – Also, we were all too nervous to run because they compare her to Kim Jong-un.
- The paragraph needs a thesis statement that relays the author's message. Sentence (5) veers from main idea.
   o **Change:** (5) into thesis statement – When leaders choose themselves to rule over people, the people often suffer due to a lack of choice, voice and representation.

The paragraph rewritten:

Our freshman class is in need of a revolution. Alice is the ninth grade's class president because there were no students who ran against her. She threatened her peers not to run, so she could run unopposed. Also, we were all too nervous to run because they compare her to Kim Jong-un. Next year, we will stage a coup, elect a new president and prevent this tragedy from happening again. When leaders choose themselves to rule over people, the people often suffer due to a lack of choice, voice and representation.

- **Correspondence** – Written communication between two or more parties.

- **Controlling Idea** – The main focus of the essay.

- **Clarity** – A characteristic of writing that effectively establishes the author's message.

- **Diction** – Words an *author* uses to convey meaning and formality to sentences. (**Think:** This instance of (formal) vs That time that (informal).)

- **Style** – Choices made by the *author* that modify the way sentences sound to the reader.

- **Coherence** – Sentences, ideas and paragraphs flow together to develop the main idea or thesis.

- **Development** – Adding details and information to support the main idea.

- **Organization** – The intentional structure of the thoughts and ideas of the writing.

- **Friendly Structure** – A more personal and informal formatting using more approachable terminology (**Think:** Exercise can be so great because it allows us to get stronger, is fun and helps with moods.)

- **Professional Structure** – A more formal and rigid formatting using more polished and conventional terminology (**Think:** Physical activity is beneficial due to its effects on muscle growth, engaging nature and positive effects on mental health.)

- **Parallel Construction** – Repeating similar word patterns to call attention to a specific idea at the word, phrase or paragraph level (**Think:** If you can write, you can edit. If you can edit, you can revise. If you can revise, you can publish. Notice the similar pattern and message throughout these sentences.)

- **Point of View** – The voice through which the writing is told (**Think:** The narrator can use 1st Person, 2nd Person, 3rd Person-limited or 3rd Person-omniscient.)

- **Annotate** – Adding notes to a text to gain understanding.

- **Paraphrase** – Using shorter phrases to summarize the main ideas to achieve clarity.

- **Commentary** – Descriptive, personal and explanatory notes on a text.

Doodles & Notes Page
Use and Enjoy

THESIS STATEMENT

The thesis statement is the most important sentence in a piece of writing. It is the main idea, the topic and the entire point for writing. Therefore, it is so important to learn how to write an effective thesis.

THESIS STATEMENT

Follow the formula below to have a solid thesis statement every time you write!

CLAIM + REASON 1 + REASON 2 + REASON 3 = THESIS

CLAIM — arguable idea the author wants the reader to accept

REASON 1 — evidence to support the claim

REASON 2 — evidence to support the claim

REASON 3 — evidence to support the claim

WRITE IT — make sure that it is well written and concise

Practice: Crazy Claims

Directions: you have been given numerous crazy claims. Try to find 3 reasons to back each up and write a thesis statement. Get creative with it!

CLAIM	REASONS	THESIS
Global warming is linked to piracy +	1. The number of pirates has decreased since the 1800s 2. Global temperatures have been steadily increasing 3. Natural disasters, such as hurricanes, have increased as well =	Since the 1800s, pirate numbers have decreased while global warming and natural disasters have increased showing that a lack of pirates causes global warming
Alligators make the best pets +	=	
The driving age should be 8 years old +	=	
Midnight snacks are the most important meal of the day +	=	

Doodles & Notes Page
Use and Enjoy

24

Read the selection, then choose and circle the best answer to each question.

Camila's teacher asked her to write an expository essay expressing her thoughts on social media. Read her paper and think about any corrections she needs to make. Once you finish reading, answer the questions that follow.

How Social Media has Affected Society

By Camila Jacobs

(1) Chances are in the last hour you've looked at your phone and checked your Tik Tok, Snapchat, Instagram or other social media platform. (2) Those offer almost unlimited opportunities for self-expression and are available worldwide. (3) But not everything that comes across a social media outlet is positive. (4) Some things in social media come across as negative. (5) The detached nature of this form of expression can lead to bullying, trolling and other negative forms of communicating with others.

(6) Social media, unlike one-sided media outlets like the newspapers, television, radio and magazines, offers two-way communication between the sender (creator of a post, blog or Tik Tok) and the receiver who views it. (7) I myself use these ways of communicating all the time. (8) As a result, people today are more aware of issues and injustices going on around them and around the world, making them more connected with their fellow man. (9) This global connection improves society as a whole's ability to work together for the common good.

(10) Older forms of communication fall short. (11) Social media shines. (12) Whether through global communication with diverse people or by helping identify people in need, improving society through awareness can be helped by social media. (13) By understanding the wonderful diversity of our global neighbors through the medium of social media, we become better. (14) Better people, better neighbors, better global citizens. (15) Let us welcome our social media platforms with open arms and embrace the positive change they have brought our society.

1 Sentence 2 is unclear. What change should Camila make to improve its clarity?

   A Change *worldwide* to **around the world**

   B Change *offer* to **offered**

   C Change *Those* to **These platforms**

   D Change *unlimited* to **endless**

E1.9(C)

2 Camila wants to rewrite sentence 7 to improve its support for topic sentence 6. Which of the following sentences would best replace sentence 7?

   F This can lead to engagement and dialogue with diverse people that was never possible in the pre-social media era.

   G I often find myself communicating with others through the use of these wonderful social media platforms.

   H Although social media can be used by everyone, it often reveals the darker side of our society and so could be harmful.

   J Sentence 7 already properly supports topic sentence 6

E1.9(C)

3 Camila may have made a mistake in organizing her first paragraph. What change, if any, should be made to correct this?

   A Move sentence 3 in front of sentence 5

   B Delete sentence 2

   C Delete sentence 4

   D No change should be made

E1.9(C)

4 Reread sentences 7 – 8. Based on these sentences only, what does it appear Camila is inferring in sentence 8?

  F People around the world are more aware of issues and connected because of her

  G People around the world are more aware of issues and connected because of social media

  H People around the world are more aware of issues and connected than they were in the past

  J People around the world are more aware of issues and connected because of their fellow man

E1.9(C)

---

5 Camila wants to change sentence 12 to the active voice to help it flow better within the paragraph. How should Camila best change this sentence to make this revision?

  A Social media helps improve society through awareness; whether through global communication with diverse people or by helping identify people in need.

  B Whether through global communication with diverse people or by helping identify people in need, social media helps improve society through awareness.

  C Improving society through awareness can be helped by social media; whether through global communication with diverse people or by helping identify people in need.

  D Whether through global communication with diverse people or by helping identify people in need, awareness of society can be improved through social media.

E1.9(C)

---

6 Camila wants to add the sentence, **Social media is better and offers many advantages over older forms of communication.**, to her essay. Where is the best place to put this sentence?

  F Before sentence 8

  G Before sentence 13

  H Before sentence 3

  J Before sentence 6

E1.9(C)

---

7 What is the best example, if any, of parallel construction within the essay?

   A Use of **social media** in every paragraph

   B Use of **negative** in the first paragraph

   C Use of **better** in the conclusion

   D Parallel construction is not used in this essay

E1.9(C)

---

8 What is the most effective way to combine sentences 10 and 11?

   F Nevertheless older forms of communication fall short, social media shines.

   G Where older forms of communication fall short, social media shines.

   H Despite older forms of communication falling short, social media shines.

   J Whenever older forms of communication fall short, social media shines.

E1.9(C)

---

9 Camila has forgotten to include a thesis statement in her introductory paragraph. Which of the following sentences best characterize the message Camila was trying to communicate?

   A Because of these potential detractors, social media hurts the growth of society with its ability to bridge the gaps of distance and open up harmful communication with diverse groups of people across the world.

   B Even with these potential detractors, social media has improved society through its ability to bridge the gaps of distance and open up communication with diverse groups of people across the world.

   C Because of these potential detractors, social media has made an impact on society through its ability to bridge the gaps of distance, and we may not be ready for open communication with diverse groups of people across the world.

   D Even with these potential detractors, social media has made an impact on society through its ability to bridge the gaps of distance, but we may not be ready for open communication with diverse groups of people across the world.

E1.9(C)

Read the selection, then choose and circle the best answer to each question.

Joseph's teacher asked him to write an expository essay expressing his thoughts on music in our lives. Read his paper and think about any corrections he needs to make. Once you finish reading, answer the questions that follow.

The Role Music Plays in our Culture and Lives

By Joseph Rodriguez

(1) Before the internet, before television, before radio, the masses found their inspiration in words. (2) Poetic texts, with their passionate reflections on life, were the voice of the young, and sometimes not so young. (3) These works were mirrors of our culture, illuminating the wonderful and awful things happening in the world around the poet. (4) Love, hate, misery, joy, corruption, redemption, all could be found in a poem. (5) That was before. (6) Before the radio brought sound to words. (7) Before the television brought face to words. (8) Before the internet brought the world together with so many voices. (9) Today we still find poems in our textbooks. (10) The voice of the young, their voice, still lyrical, is now musical. (11) Music now gives voice to today's global generation, providing for the expression of their struggles and for everything from when they are born to when they struggle with their lives.

(12) If you ask the youth of today how many of them read the newspaper that morning, I'm sure the number would be small. (13) But if you asked the youth of today, how many listened to music that morning, I believe the number would be much larger. (14) It's on our radios; it's in our videos; it's in our wireless earbuds; it's on our Bluetooth speakers. (15) I know it's on mine. (16) Music is intertwined as a universal language across cultures around the globe. (17) Music even covers everything we're going through. (18) When we're angry, we listen to angry music. (19) When we're sad, we listen to sad music. (20) When we're bored, we listen to uplifting music. (21) Music is our voice and we express all these feelings by singing along.

(22) For me personally I believe in the enormous, intertwined and the universal role music plays in our lives, in our society, and in our culture. (23) This role that music plays today in our culture cannot be overstated. (24) It provides a voice to the masses. (25) It creates a bridge of understanding across cultural divides. (26) It offers an endless form of expression.

(27) Today's youth hasn't lost the passion that was once found mostly in poetry of old, we simply replaced the delivery system with something better: music.

1 Joseph wants to add the dependent clause, **limited only by our imagination and experiences** to his essay. Where is the best place to add this clause?

   A To the beginning of sentence 2

   B To the end of sentence 26

   C After **their voice,** in sentence 10

   D To the beginning of sentence 16

E1.9(C)

2 Joseph would like to add the phrase, **Music, as a medium to express and exchange ideas, is stronger than written words.**, to strengthen his essay. Where should he add this phrase to best increase the coherence of his overall essay?

   F Before sentence 1

   G Before sentence 10

   H Before sentence 12

   J Before sentence 22

E1.9(C)

3 Which of the following is an example of parallel construction?

   A Sentences 6 - 8

   B Sentences 18 - 20

   C Sentences 24 - 26

   D All of the above

E1.9(C)

4 Joseph is worried his thesis sentence doesn't capture his main idea properly. What sentence below, if any, improves his thesis sentence succinctly and accurately to reflect his main ideas?

F Music is a forum for today's generation and is better than poetry for letting people express how they feel.

G Music now gives voice to today's generation and their struggles, providing for expression of everything from when they are born to when they struggle with life.

H Music now gives voice to today's generation and their struggles, providing an endless forum for the expression of everything from birth to death.

J No change, the current thesis sentence already properly and succinctly reflects all main ideas

E1.9(C)

---

5 What change, if any, should Joseph make to improve the diction of sentence 22?

A Remove the words **for me personally**

B Add a comma after **for me personally**

C Add a semicolon after **for me personally**

D No change should be made

E1.9(C)

---

6 After re-reading his introductory paragraph, Joseph believes sentences 9 and 10 sound stilted and should be combined. What is the best way to combine these sentences?

F Today we still find poems in our textbooks, and the voice of the young, their voice, still lyrical, is now musical.

G Today we still find poems in our textbooks, as if the voice of the young, their voice, still lyrical, is now musical.

H Today we still find poems in our textbooks, where the voice of the young, their voice, still lyrical, is now musical.

J Today we still find poems in our textbooks, but the voice of the young, their voice, still lyrical, is now musical.

E1.9(C)

7 Joseph made a mistake organizing the second paragraph. What change should he make to correct this error?

   A Move sentence 17 before sentence 14

   B Move sentence 16 before sentence 14

   C Move sentence 21 before sentence 18

   D Move sentence 20 before sentence 18

E1.9(C)

---

8 Joseph worries that sentence 14 doesn't deliver his message effectively. What change, if any, would you make to sentence 14 to improve its clarity?

   F Change the first *it's* to **music is**

   G Change both occurrences of the word *in* to **on**

   H Change the semicolons to commas

   J No change is needed

E1.9(C)

---

9 What sentence in the second paragraph does not add to its development?

   A Sentence 13

   B Sentence 15

   C Sentence 17

   D Sentence 20

E1.9(C)

Testing TIPS Navigating the Expository Essay

The English I STAAR Essay is expository. This means you must explain an idea in thorough detail with examples to back it up. Evaluators are looking for organization, a clear thesis, good word choice and focus.

Example Prompt

The 'quote' and the 'think' statements are distractors – Circle "write an essay about" and focus on only that as your essay topic.

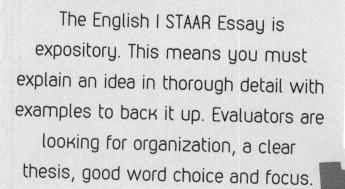

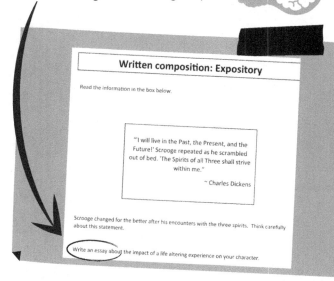

Written composition: Expository

Read the information in the box below.

> "'I will live in the Past, the Present, and the Future!' Scrooge repeated as he scrambled out of bed. 'The Spirits of all Three shall strive within me."
>
> ~ Charles Dickens

Scrooge changed for the better after his encounters with the three spirits. Think carefully about this statement.

Write an essay about the impact of a life altering experience on your character.

Organizing Your Essay

1. Introductory Paragraph: hook, transition, thesis
2. Body Paragraph: topic sentence, supporting examples that link back to the thesis
3. Conclusion: sum up essay, restates thesis in a new way, ends with a thought provoking statement

Doodles & Notes Page
Use and Enjoy

Written composition: Expository

Read the information in the box below.

> "We shall fight on the beaches, we shall fight on the landing-grounds, we shall fight in the fields and in the streets, we shall fight in the hills. We shall never surrender!"."
>
> ~ Winston Churchill

People have been known to explore their limits. Think carefully about this statement.

Write an essay about the lengths someone will go to survive in a crisis.

Be sure to –

- Clearly state your Thesis
- Organize and Develop your Ideas effectively
- Choose your Words carefully
- Edit your writing for Grammar, Mechanics and Spelling

Helpful Hint: Use this sheet for notes and to gather your thoughts before starting the essay — just like you should on the STAAR.

DO NOT WRITE OUTSIDE THE BOX PROVIDED

FICTION

Defining the Genre and Genre Characteristics:

When we think of literature, our first thought often goes to Fiction. But why is that? Fiction encompasses our fantasies, imagination, dreams and hopes while connecting to our realities using dynamic characters and captivating situations.

Fiction is any creative work that is not based strictly on facts and history, but encompasses imagined story elements.

You know a story is Fictional if it:

- Describes imaginary events, people or places
- May be based on reality with fabricated characters, situations or settings
- Follows common archetypal story structures (**Think:** Hero's Journey, Battle between Good and Evil, Coming of Age, Rags to Riches, etc.)
- Focuses on dynamic, often exaggerated, character narratives
- Has a strong use of imagery, symbolism and expressive language
- Readers must infer the theme or message from the author, often through the character's actions and understanding of the world around them

Examples of Fictional Novels for High School Readers:

- *The Great Gatsby* by F. Scott Fitzgerald
- *The Fault in our Stars* by John Green
- *Dracula* by Bram Stoker
- *The Hate You Give* by Angie Thomas
- *Lord of the Flies* by William Golding
- *The Shining* by Stephen King
- *Lovely Bones* by Alice Sebold

Doodles & Notes Page
Use and Enjoy

40

- **Author's Purpose** – An author's reason for writing (**Think:** P.I.E. – Persuade, Inform, Entertain.)

- **Theme** – The message or moral of the story.

- **Setting** – The time and place where a story takes place.

- **Mood** – The atmosphere and overall feeling an artistic work conveys to the reader (**Think:** How the reader feels.)

- **Tone** – The writer's point of view towards the subject of the artistic work (**Think:** How the author feels.)

- **Plot** – Sequence of events in a story.

  - **Linear plot** – A plot that has a clear beginning, middle and end and follows the order: Exposition – Rising Action – Climax – Falling Action – Resolution.

  - **Non-linear plot** – A plot that is out of chronological order.

    - **Unresolved** – The story has no, or is missing, the Resolution. The conflict remains unfinished.

    - **Flashback** – Scenes that take place before (or go back to earlier events within) the story.

    - **Foreshadow** – The author hints at events yet to come in the story.

    - **Parallel plot** – Two or more main stories that are connected through a common location, character or theme. The story will often bounce between story lines and merge together at the Resolution.

  - **Subplot** – A side-story that helps define the main story or characters reactions to events.

- **Characterization** – How the author constructs and describes a character's traits.

- **Character foil** – A character that has opposite traits or characteristics from another character, typically the protagonist (the main character.)

- **Conflict** – A struggle between two or more forces within the story. Can be conflicts between characters, within a character's own mind, Nature, Society, etc. (**Think:** Man vs Man, Man vs Self, Man vs Nature, Man vs Society, Man vs Supernatural, etc.)
- **Narrator** – the voice of the story; the person who delivers commentary on the book's events (can be in 1st Person, 2nd Person, 3rd Person-limited or 3rd Person-omniscient.)
  - **1st Person Narrator** – A character is telling the story from their own point of view (Identified by "I", "Me" and "We" statements.)
  - **2nd Person Narrator** – The narrator speaks directly to the readers (Identified by "You", "Your" and "Yours" statements.)
  - **3rd Person-limited Narrator** – An external narrator tells the story based on what has been revealed to them (Identified by "He", "She", and "They" statements.)
  - **3rd Person-omniscient Narrator** – An external narrator tells the story with knowledge of everything around and within the story (Identified by "He", "She", and "They" statements.)
- **Figurative language** – Phrasing that goes beyond the literal definition and evokes an emotional response to deliver the author's message.
- **Irony** – Literary device that contrasts expectation and reality. Usually, the results are the opposite of expectations.
  - **Dramatic Irony** – When the reader knows something the characters don't (**Think:** A thriller where we know the killer is behind the door, but the character does not know and opens the door.)
  - **Situational Irony** – When the reader expects one outcome, but the opposite happens (**Think:** A character stays up all night studying for the most important test of their life, then sleeps through their alarm and misses the test.)
  - **Verbal Irony** – A character says one thing, but means the opposite, often expressed as sarcasm (**Think:** A character trips over a backpack and makes a mess, then another character says, "Nice move, Grace.".)
- **Compare** – Describing the similarities between two or more topics.
- **Contrast** – Describing the differences between two or more topics.

CHARACTERIZATION

Authors use Direct and Indirect Characterization to describe their characters. Direct Characterization is when an author directly tells the reader a character's traits (Susy was a sour, spoiled little girl with an attitude.) Indirect Characterization is when the author shows the reader a character's traits through that character's thoughts, actions and dialogue (Susy stomped her foot and screeched, "I want it now!")

USING S.T.E.A.L. WITH INDIRECT CHARACTERIZATION

Identify the following details and determine how they contribute to a character's traits.

SPEECH

THOUGHTS

EFFECTS ON OTHERS

ACTIONS

LOOKS

Practice: Character Chart

Directions: choose your favorite movie or book character and use S.T.E.A.L. to characterize them

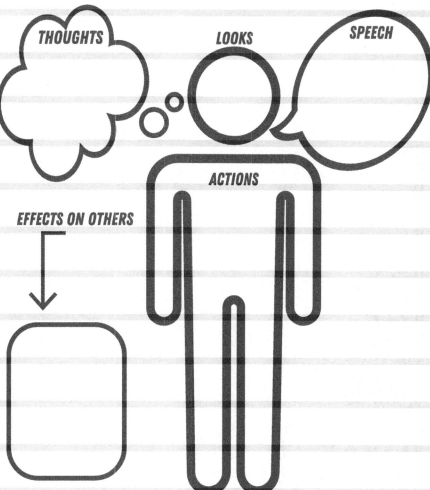

Doodles & Notes Page
Use and Enjoy

Read the selection, then choose and circle the best answer to each question.

from

A Christmas Carol

By Charles Dickens

(1) At last, however, he began to think—as you or I would have thought at first; for it is always the person not in the predicament who knows what ought to have been done in it, and would unquestionably have done it too—at last, I say, he began to think that the source and secret of this ghostly light might be in the adjoining room, from whence, on further tracing it, it seemed to shine. (2) This idea taking full possession of his mind, he got up softly, and shuffled in his slippers to the door.

(3) The moment Scrooge's hand was on the lock a strange voice called him by his name, and bade him enter. (4) He obeyed.

(5) It was his own room. (6) There was no doubt about that. (7) But it had undergone a surprising transformation. (8) The walls and ceiling were so hung with living green, that it looked a perfect grove; from every part of which bright gleaming berries glistened. (9) The crisp leaves of holly, mistletoe, and ivy reflected back the light, as if so many little mirrors had been scattered there; and such a mighty blaze went roaring up the chimney as that dull petrification of a hearth had never known in Scrooge's time, or Marley's, or for many and many a winter season gone. (10) Heaped up on the floor, to form a kind of throne, were turkeys, geese, game, poultry, brawn, great joints of meat, sucking-pigs, long wreaths of sausages, mince-pies, plum-puddings, barrels of oysters, red-hot chestnuts, cherry-cheeked apples, juicy oranges, luscious pears, immense twelfth-cakes, and seething bowls of punch, that made the chamber dim with their delicious steam. (11) In easy state upon this couch there sat a jolly Giant, glorious to see; who bore a glowing torch, in shape not unlike Plenty's horn, and held it up, high up, to shed its light on Scrooge as he came peeping round the door.

(12) 'Come in!' exclaimed the Ghost. (13) 'Come in! and know me better, man!'

(14) Scrooge entered timidly, and hung his head before this Spirit. (15) He was not the dogged Scrooge he had been; and though the Spirit's eyes were clear and kind, he did not like to meet them.

(16) 'I am the Ghost of Christmas Present,' said the Spirit. (17) 'Look upon me!'

(18) Scrooge reverently did so. (19) It was clothed in one simple deep green robe, or mantle, bordered with white fur. (20) This garment hung so loosely on the figure, that its capacious breast was bare, as if disdaining to be warded or concealed by any artifice. (21) Its feet, observable beneath the ample folds of the garment, were also bare; and on its head it wore no other covering than a holly wreath, set here and there with shining icicles. (22) Its dark-brown curls were long and free; free as its genial face, its sparkling eye, its open hand, its cheery voice, its unconstrained demeanour, and its joyful air. (23) Girded round its middle was an antique scabbard: but no sword was in it, and the ancient sheath was eaten up with rust.

...

(24) The bell struck Twelve.

(25) Scrooge looked about him for the Ghost, and saw it not. (26) As the last stroke ceased to vibrate, he remembered the prediction of old Jacob Marley, and, lifting up his eyes, beheld a solemn Phantom, draped and hooded, coming like a mist along the ground towards him.

(27) The Phantom slowly, gravely, silently approached. (28) When it came near him, Scrooge bent down upon his knee; for in the very air through which this Spirit moved it seemed to scatter gloom and mystery.

(29) It was shrouded in a deep black garment, which concealed its head, its face, its form, and left nothing of it visible, save one outstretched hand. (30) But for this, it would have been difficult to detach its figure from the night, and separate it from the darkness by which it was surrounded.

(31) He felt that it was tall and stately when it came beside him, and that its mysterious presence filled him with a solemn dread. (32) He knew no more, for the Spirit neither spoke nor moved.

(33) 'I am in the presence of the Ghost of Christmas Yet to Come?' said Scrooge.

(34) The Spirit answered not, but pointed onward with its hand.

(35) 'You are about to show me shadows of the things that have not happened, but will happen in the time before us,' Scrooge pursued. (36) 'Is that so, Spirit?'

(37) The upper portion of the garment was contracted for an instant in its folds, as if the Spirit had inclined its head. (38) That was the only answer he received.

(39) Although well used to ghostly company by this time, Scrooge feared the silent shape so much that his legs trembled beneath him, and he found that he could hardly stand when he prepared to follow it. (40) The Spirit paused a moment, as observing his condition, and giving him time to recover.

(41) But Scrooge was all the worse for this. (42) It thrilled him with a vague, uncertain horror to know that, behind the dusky shroud, there were ghostly eyes intently fixed upon him, while he, though he stretched his own to the utmost, could see nothing but a spectral hand and one great heap of black.

(43) 'Ghost of the Future!' he exclaimed, 'I fear you more than any spectre I have seen. (44) But as I know your purpose is to do me good, and as I hope to live to be another man from what I was, I am prepared to bear your company, and do it with a thankful heart. (45) Will you not speak to me?'

(46) It gave him no reply. (47) The hand was pointed straight before them.

(48) 'Lead on!' said Scrooge. (49) 'Lead on! (50) The night is waning fast, and it is precious time to me, I know. (51) Lead on, Spirit!'

(52) The Phantom moved away as it had come towards him. (53) Scrooge followed in the shadow of its dress, which bore him up, he thought, and carried him along.

Fiction: Questions Part 1 – from *A Christmas Carol*

> "But for this, it would have been difficult to detach its figure from the night, and separate it from the darkness by which it was surrounded. He felt that it was tall and stately when it came beside him, and that its mysterious presence filled him with a solemn dread."

1 Based on this quotation from the reading passage, what can be inferred about the Ghost of Christmas Yet to Come?

   A   The spirit is aggressive and menacing

   B   The spirit is verbose and affable

   C   The spirit is an ominous enigma

   D   The spirit is genial and sympathetic

E1.6(B)

---

2 In Lines 8-10, the mood of the scene can best be described as –

   F   gloomy

   G   peaceful

   H   nostalgic

   J   festive

E1.6(D)

---

3 By using the word, "shuffled" in Line 2, the author establishes Scrooge as being –

   A   apprehensive

   B   clumsy

   C   panic-stricken

   D   jubilous

E1.8(D)

> "It is always the person not in the predicament who knows what ought to have been done in it."

4 The irony of this quotation is that it calls attention to –

   F people's tendency to assume they know what others should do

   G hindsight always being 20-20

   H Scrooge being in a predicament

   J Scrooge's understanding of what should be done

E1.8(E)

---

5 In Line 9, Dickens' description of a hearth known in Scrooge's time shows the author finds Scrooge to be –

   A calculating

   B impoverished

   C unintelligent

   D cold-hearted

E1.8(F)

---

6 In Line 27, the word, "Gravely" most likely means what?

   F Ghostly

   G Somberly

   H Importantly

   J Stately

E1.2(B)

---

7 In Line 14, what is the closet definition to the word, "Dogged"?

    A Determined, thorough

    B Obstinate, pertinacious

    C Rude, chivalrous

    D Tenacious, hardworking

E1.2

---

8 Based on the passage, what can be inferred about Scrooge's situation?

    F Scrooge lives in a haunted house

    G The spirits visit Scrooge to terrify him

    H The spirits visit Scrooge to encourage change

    J Scrooge has accidentally summoned two ghosts

E1.4

---

9 In Line 26, by comparing the phantom to mist, the author is attempting to –

    A use concrete details to describe the spirit

    B show that the spirit is transparent

    C describe the ghostly visage through sensory details

    D personify mist to be phantom-like

E1.8(D)

MINDFUL
moment

"The creation of a thousand forests is in one acorn."
~ Ralph Waldo Emerson

Mindful doodling can be a lot of fun and is a relaxing way to relieve stress. We have included some example patterns and doodles for you, but you can doodle whatever pattern you'd like. It's all about taking a break, not stressing about it. We have also included many pages throughout this book for you to take notes or just take a break and doodle!

Doodles & Notes Page
Use and Enjoy

52

Read the selection, then choose and circle the best answer to each question.

From

Frankenstein

By Mary Shelley

(1) It was on a dreary night of November that I beheld the accomplishment of my toils. (2) With an anxiety that almost amounted to agony, I collected the instruments of life around me, that I might infuse a spark of being into the lifeless thing that lay at my feet. (3) It was already one in the morning; the rain pattered dismally against the panes, and my candle was nearly burnt out, when, by the glimmer of the half-extinguished light, I saw the dull yellow eye of the creature open; it breathed hard, and a convulsive motion agitated its limbs.

(4) How can I describe my emotions at this catastrophe, or how delineate the wretch whom with such infinite pains and care I had endeavoured to form? (5) His limbs were in proportion, and I had selected his features as beautiful. (6) Beautiful! (7) Great God! (8) His yellow skin scarcely covered the work of muscles and arteries beneath; his hair was of a lustrous black, and flowing; his teeth of a pearly whiteness; but these luxuriances only formed a more horrid contrast with his watery eyes, that seemed almost of the same colour as the dun-white sockets in which they were set, his shrivelled complexion and straight black lips.

(9) The different accidents of life are not so changeable as the feelings of human nature. (10) I had worked hard for nearly two years, for the sole purpose of infusing life into an inanimate body. (11) For this I had deprived myself of rest and health. (12) I had desired it with an ardour that far exceeded moderation; but now that I had finished, the beauty of the dream vanished, and breathless horror and disgust filled my heart. (13) Unable to endure the aspect of the being I had created, I rushed out of the room and continued a long time traversing my bed-chamber, unable to compose my mind to sleep. (14) At length lassitude succeeded to the tumult I had before endured, and I threw myself on the bed in my clothes, endeavouring to seek a few moments of forgetfulness. (15) But it was in vain; I slept, indeed, but I was disturbed by the wildest dreams.

(16) I thought I saw Elizabeth, in the bloom of health, walking in the streets of Ingolstadt. (17) Delighted and surprised, I embraced her, but as I imprinted the first kiss on her lips, they became livid with the hue of death; her features appeared to change, and I thought that I held the corpse of my dead mother in my arms; a shroud enveloped her form, and I saw the grave-worms crawling in the folds of the flannel. (18) I started from my sleep with horror; a cold dew covered my forehead, my teeth chattered, and every limb became convulsed; when, by the dim and yellow light of the moon, as it forced its way through the window shutters, I beheld the wretch—the miserable monster whom I had created. (19) He held up the curtain of the bed; and his eyes, if eyes they may be called, were fixed on me. (20) His jaws opened, and he muttered some inarticulate sounds, while a grin wrinkled his cheeks. (21) He might have spoken, but I did not hear; one hand was stretched out, seemingly to detain me, but I escaped and rushed downstairs. (22) I took refuge in the courtyard belonging to the house which I inhabited, where I remained during the rest of the night, walking up and down in the greatest agitation, listening attentively, catching and fearing each sound as if it were to announce the approach of the demoniacal corpse to which I had so miserably given life.

(23) Oh! (24) No mortal could support the horror of that countenance. (25) A mummy again endued with animation could not be so hideous as that wretch. (26) I had gazed on him while unfinished; he was ugly then, but when those muscles and joints were rendered capable of motion, it became a thing such as even Dante could not have conceived.

Fiction: Questions Part 2 – from *Frankenstein*

1 One can infer from this selection that the author's purpose for writing *Frankenstein* was to –

   A entertain

   B inform

   C educate

   D persuade

E1.8(A)

2 The narrator's horror at his creation supports the author's message that –

   F people can do anything that they put their mind to if they try

   G science experiments can go horribly wrong

   H new technology can be formed from old mistakes

   J you must consider the consequences before acting

E1.8(D)

3 Which line in the passage best describes the setting?

   A Line 9

   B Line 3

   C Line 18

   D Line 13

E1.6(D)

"I started from my sleep with horror; a cold dew covered my forehead, my teeth chattered, and every limb became convulsed; when, by the dim and yellow light of the moon, as it forced its way through the window shutters, I beheld the wretch—the miserable monster whom I had created."

4 This quotation contributes to which of the following moods?

  F Sorrowful and sanguine

  G Foreboding and regretful

  H Angry and dejected

  J Terse and choleric

E1.8(F)

5 The author uses overstatement in Lines 24-26 to achieve what purpose?

  A To show the dramatic tendencies of the narrator

  B To compare the creature's malevolent nature to the narrator's nature

  C To describe the narrator's view of the monstrosity of the creature

  D To illuminate the narrator's intense fear

E1.8(G)

6 The author uses a simile in Line 9 to communicate what to the reader?

  F Accidents in life are similar to human feelings

  G Mistakes cannot be easily reversed

  H Errors can change human emotions

  J Flaws are the result of human passions

E1.6

7 This passage is a work of fiction characterized by all of the following except –

   A the reader must infer the theme from the author's words

   B it is based in reality with fabricated elements

   C it has multiple, clear supporting details to develop a claim

   D it uses strong imagery and symbolism

E1.7

---

8 Which of the following inferences can be made on the significance of the narrator's dream in Lines 15-17?

   F The narrator misses Elizabeth

   G The creature reminds the narrator of his mother

   H Elizabeth will be horrified by the creature

   J Elizabeth's death is foreshadowed

E1.4(F)

Testing TIPS

How to Score Your Expository Essay

Your English I STAAR Essay will be rated by two independent educators. You can receive a 1, 2, 3 or 4 with 4 being the highest rating. A 4 essay will be organized, structurally sound, focused, will follow the prompt and will have a clear, defined thesis.

Self Evaluation Time

Remember the tips from the STAAR prompt. Now it's time to go back to grade and evaluate your completed essays using the STAAR Checklist

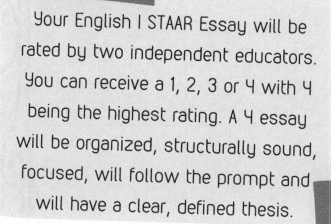

Scoring Your Essay

STAAR CHECKLIST

Expository Essay

	Yes	No	
Is there a clear thesis that restates and specifically addresses the prompt?	☐	☐ →	1
Does the writer attempt to develop ideas? (Avoids repetition)	☐	☐ →	1
Writing errors do not severely impact the fluency of the essay.	☐	☐ →	1
Ideas are well connected and address the writer's topic.	☐	☐ →	2
Writer supports thesis with SPECIFIC persuasive evidence THROUGHOUT.	☐	☐ →	2
Can the essay be read smoothly?	☐	☐ →	2
Writer provides unique viewpoints/reflections.	☐	☐ →	3
Writer uses strong diction to promote purpose.	☐	☐ →	3
Sentence variety is used effectively.	☐	☐ →	3
			4

Be sure to –

- Clearly state your <u>Thesis</u>
- <u>Organize</u> and <u>Develop</u> your <u>Ideas</u> effectively
- <u>Choose</u> your <u>Words</u> carefully
- <u>Edit</u> your writing for <u>Grammar</u>, <u>Mechanics</u> and <u>Spelling</u>

A full size version of this Checklist has been provided on the back of all following essay pages in the book.

Doodles & Notes Page
Use and Enjoy

Written composition: Expository

Read the information in the box below.

> "'I will live in the Past, the Present, and the Future!' Scrooge repeated as he scrambled out of bed. 'The Spirits of all Three shall strive within me."
>
> ~ Charles Dickens

Scrooge changed for the better after his encounters with the three spirits. Think carefully about this statement.

Write an essay about the impact of a life altering experience on your character.

Be sure to –

- Clearly state your <u>Thesis</u>
- <u>Organize</u> and <u>Develop</u> your <u>Ideas</u> effectively
- <u>Choose</u> your <u>Words</u> carefully
- <u>Edit</u> your writing for <u>Grammar</u>, <u>Mechanics</u> and <u>Spelling</u>

Helpful Hint: Use this sheet for notes and to gather your thoughts before starting the essay – just like you should on the STAAR.

DO NOT WRITE OUTSIDE THE BOX PROVIDED

STAAR CHECKLIST

Expository Essay

	Yes	No	
Is there a clear thesis that restates and specifically addresses the prompt?	☐	☐	→ 1
↓			
Does the writer attempt to develop ideas? (Avoids repetition)	☐	☐	→ 1
↓			
Writing errors do not severely impact the fluency of the essay.	☐	☐	→ 1
↓			
Ideas are well connected and address the writer's topic.	☐	☐	→ 2
↓			
Writer supports thesis with SPECIFIC persuasive evidence THROUGHOUT.	☐	☐	→ 2
↓			
Can the essay be read smoothly?	☐	☐	→ 2
↓			
Writer provides unique viewpoints/reflections.	☐	☐	→ 3
↓			
Writer uses strong diction to promote purpose.	☐	☐	→ 3
↓			
Sentence variety is used effectively.	☐	☐	→ 3
↓			

Don't Forget to go back and grade your 1st Essay!   **4**

64

Defining the Genre and Genre Characteristics:

Poetry, ugh... That might be your first thought. However, some of the most expressive language ever written can be found in poems. From great poets like Robert Frost, Shel Silverstein, Emily Dickenson, Edgar Allan Poe and more, you can find poetry encompassing every subject and every style of writing.

Poetry is a creative work that focuses on self-expression through a distinct style, meter and rhythm with an emphasis on emotion, figurative language and sounds.

You can identify a Poem if it:

- Uses Rhyme or Rhythm to produce certain effects
- Is very Descriptive and uses Vivid Figurative Language
- Has Punction and Formatting arranged in unconventional ways that manipulate how the words sound or look to better express the Poet's intent
- Often covers topics such as, Romantic Love, Nature, Emotional Expression, etc.
- Strong use of imagery, symbolism and expressive language
- Readers must infer the theme or message from the poet, often through the figurative meaning, punction and the shape of the text on the page

Examples of Poetry for High School Readers:

- "The Raven" by Edgar Allan Poe
- "Because I Could Not Stop for Death" by Emily Dickenson
- "We Real Cool" by Gwendolyn Brooks
- "Do Not Go Gentle into that Good Night" by Dillon Thomas
- "Jaberwocky" by Lewis Carrol
- "Fire and Ice" by Robert Frost
- "Where the Sidewalk Ends" by Shel Silverstein

Doodles & Notes Page
Use and Enjoy

- **Audience** – Intended readers of a piece of writing.

- **Message** – What the writer is trying to communicate to the reader.

- **Line** – A single row in a poem that ends for a reason other than the margins on the page. The reason for this break could be so the row has a certain number of syllables, stresses, to rhyme, or simply because the poet wanted to end at that point.

- **Stanza** – A group of Lines in a poem structured according to the intent of the poem to form meanings. These can be 2, 3, 4, 5 or more grouped lines based on the poet's desires.
    - **Couplet** – A two Line stanza.
    - **Tercet** – A three Line stanza.
    - **Quatrain** – A four Line stanza.

- **Rhyme Scheme** – The pattern of rhymes occurring at the end of a poem (**Think:** 6 lines ending in: cat, bat, cow, shoe, now, glue is a Rhyme Scheme of AABCBC. **Note:** Each new sounding ending within a stanza changes the alphabetical identification of the end rhyme. **Example:** If the 'Think' example was changed to: cat, cow, shoe, bat, now, brown, then the Rhyme Scheme would change to ABCABD.)

- **Voice** – A writer's unique style of writing that enables the expression of their personality.

- **Diction** – The word choices an author or poet makes to establish their message.

- **Prosody** – Examining the rhythm, meter, tempo and other structural elements of a poetic work.

- **Explicit** – The text is stated clearly with no confusion on intent of meaning.

- **Implicit** – The text uses metaphorical language that requires inference.

- **Overstatement** – Making an exaggeration (**Think:** I am starving when you're just hungry).

- **Understatement** – Saying something is less than what it is (**Think:** It's only a flesh wound when it's really a mortal blow).

- **Oxymoron** – Two words with opposite meanings combined to create new meaning (**Think:** Jumbo shrimp; Pretty ugly; Original copy; Deafening silence).

- **Analogy** – Compares two like things with the goal of relaying a message (**Think:** Comparing yourself to a bee to show you are busy).

67

- **Alliteration** – The repetition of like sounds.

  o **Assonance** – Repetitive vowel sounds at the start, middle or end of words (**Think:** He fell Asleep in a Tree).

  o **Consonance** – Repetitive consonant sounds at the start, middle or end of words (**Think:** Sally Sells Sea Shells).

FIGURATIVE LANGUAGE

Poets use figurative language to relay their ideas and themes in sensory ways. The key to understanding these literary phrases is to not take them literally but focus on context and a deeper meaning. Sometimes, this means you'll have to make inferences!

TYPES OF FIGURATIVE LANGUAGE:

See definitions and examples below.

METAPHOR: A DIRECT COMPARISON OF TWO THINGS

ex: this <u>room</u> is an <u>oven</u>

SIMILE: A COMPARISON OF TWO THINGS USING LIKE OR AS

ex: <u>she</u> shines <u>like</u> the <u>sun</u>

IDIOM: A COMMON PHRASE WITH A DIFFERING FIGURATIVE MEANING

ex: <u>spill the tea</u>

HYPERBOLE: AN EXTREME EXAGGERATION

ex: I am <u>literally freezing</u>

ALLUSION: A SUBTLE REFERENCE

ex: he is such a <u>Romeo</u> with the ladies

PERSONIFICATION: GIVING HUMAN CHARACTERISTICS TO SOMETHING NONHUMAN

ex: the <u>waves called</u> to me

Practice: Literary Memes

Directions: create a meme for each of the types of figurative language

METAPHOR

Look: a meme that's a metaphor for my life!

SIMILE

IDIOM

HYPERBOLE

ALLUSION

PERSONIFICATION

69

Doodles & Notes Page
Use and Enjoy

70

Read the selection, then choose and circle the best answer to each question.

If...

By Rudyard Kipling

If you can keep your head when all about you

Are losing theirs and blaming it on you,

If you can trust yourself when all men doubt you,

But make allowance for their doubting too;

(5)   If you can wait and not be tired by waiting,

Or being lied about, don't deal in lies,

Or being hated, don't give way to hating,

And yet don't look too good, nor talk too wise:

If you can dream—and not make dreams your master;

(10)   If you can think—and not make thoughts your aim;

If you can meet with Triumph and Disaster

And treat those two impostors just the same;

If you can bear to hear the truth you've spoken

Twisted by knaves to make a trap for fools,

(15)   Or watch the things you gave your life to, broken,

And stoop and build 'em up with worn-out tools:

If you can make one heap of all your winnings

And risk it on one turn of pitch-and-toss,

And lose, and start again at your beginnings

(20)   And never breathe a word about your loss;

If you can force your heart and nerve and sinew

To serve your turn long after they are gone,

And so hold on when there is nothing in you

Except the Will which says to them: 'Hold on!'

(25) If you can talk with crowds and keep your virtue,

Or walk with Kings—nor lose the common touch,

If neither foes nor loving friends can hurt you,

If all men count with you, but none too much;

If you can fill the unforgiving minute

(30) With sixty seconds' worth of distance run,

Yours is the Earth and everything that's in it,

And—which is more—you'll be a Man, my son!

Poetry: Questions Part 1 – from "If…"

1   What is the narrator's tone towards his intended audience?

   A   Protective, fatherly

   B   Pretentious, genuine

   C   Warm, affable

   D   Polite, enthusiastic

E1.8(F)

2   What is the purpose of the author's repetition of the word 'if' in the poem?

   F   It suggest the narrator's advice is unnecessary

   G   It highlights the narrator's fear for the audience's future

   H   It emphasizes what the audience must do

   J   It highlights the unlikeliness of the audience's success

E1.7(B)

> If you can think—and not make thoughts your aim;
>
> If you can meet with Triumph and Disaster
>
> And treat those two impostors just the same;
>
> If you can bear to hear the truth you've spoken

3   What does the poet personify in this quotation?

   A   Thoughts

   B   Truth

   C   Two imposters

   D   Triumph and Disaster

E1.8(E)

4 What is the rhyme scheme of Stanza 4?

    F A, A, B, B, C, C, D, D

    G A, B, A, B, C, D, C, D

    H A, B, B, A, C, D, C, D

    J A, B, C, A, B, C, D, D

E1.8

5 What aspect of life is referenced in Lines 13-16?

    A Challenges, distractions

    B Love, camaraderie

    C Old age, death

    D Defeat, loss

E1.4(E)

6 What is the symbolic meaning of "heart and nerve and sinew" on Line 21 of the poem?

    F Hope and determination and strength

    G Romance and intelligence and ferocity

    H Courage and attitude and health

    J Love and confidence and muscle

E1.4(D)

"Peace comes from within, do not seek it without"
~ Buddha

Within the rows and columns are 9 moon phases. You will fill out the dotted boxes with the missing moons without repeating any in the solid boxes, columns or rows

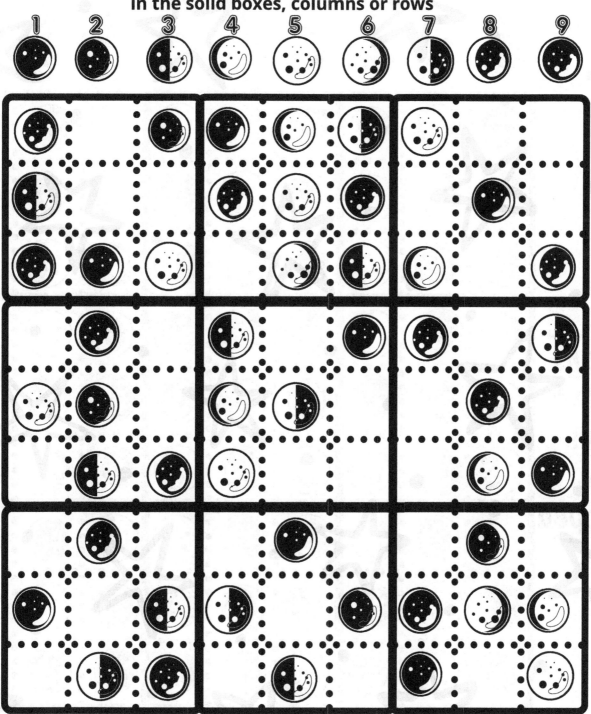

Mindful Moons Solution

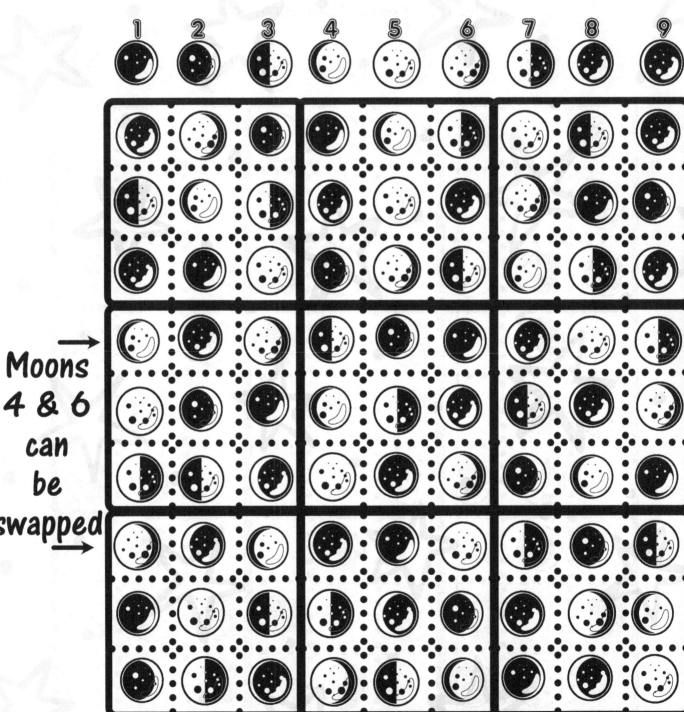

Moons 4 & 6 can be swapped

Read the selection, then choose and circle the best answer to each question.

Annabel Lee

By Edgar Allan Poe

It was many and many a year ago,

In a kingdom by the sea,

That a maiden there lived whom you may know

By the name of Annabel Lee;

(5)   And this maiden she lived with no other thought

Than to love and be loved by me.

I was a child and she was a child,

In this kingdom by the sea,

But we loved with a love that was more than love—

(10)   I and my Annabel Lee—

With a love that the wingèd seraphs of Heaven

Coveted her and me.

And this was the reason that, long ago,

In this kingdom by the sea,

(15)   A wind blew out of a cloud, chilling

My beautiful Annabel Lee;

So that her highborn kinsmen came

And bore her away from me,

To shut her up in a sepulchre

(20)   In this kingdom by the sea.

The angels, not half so happy in Heaven,

Went envying her and me—

Yes!—that was the reason (as all men know,

In this kingdom by the sea)

(25)   That the wind came out of the cloud by night,

Chilling and killing my Annabel Lee.

But our love it was stronger by far than the love

Of those who were older than we—

Of many far wiser than we—

(30)   And neither the angels in Heaven above

Nor the demons down under the sea

Can ever dissever my soul from the soul

Of the beautiful Annabel Lee;

For the moon never beams, without bringing me dreams

(35)   Of the beautiful Annabel Lee;

And the stars never rise, but I feel the bright eyes

Of the beautiful Annabel Lee;

And so, all the night-tide, I lie down by the side

Of my darling—my darling—my life and my bride,

(40)   In her sepulchre there by the sea—

In her tomb by the sounding sea.

Poetry: Questions Part 2 – from "Annabel Lee"

1 Which lines in the poem best highlight the narrator's obsession with Annabel Lee?

   A Lines 38 - 39

   B Lines 5 - 6

   C Lines 15 - 16

   D Lines 27 - 28

E1.8(D)

2 The narrator's reference to Annabel's kinsmen as "highborn" implies that –

   F he is highborn as well and is deserving of respect

   G Annabel Lee rules the kingdom they live in

   H they did not approve of his relationship with Annabel Lee

   J he is lowborn and should be pitied

E1.8(F)

3 The narrator mentions "wingèd seraphs." What is a synonym for seraph?

   A Deity

   B Angel

   C Demon

   D Spirit

E1.2(A)

4 Based on the poem, what can we infer the narrator believes killed Annabel Lee?

   F The kinsmen

   G The plague

   H The wind

   J The angels

E1.2(B)

5 Which of the following statements would the narrator most likely agree with?

   A Love is more painful than death

   B Love ends with death

   C Love never dies

   D Love and death are interchangeable

E1.8(A)

6 What can the reader infer as to the true cause of Annabel's death?

   F Hypothermia

   G Supernatural forces

   H Jealous angels

   J Cold wind

E1.4(F)

80

Testing TIPS How to Identify Question Distractors

Multiple-choice questions are made up of at least two parts – the correct answer and one or more distractors. The difference between passing and excelling is largely based on your knowledge and your ability to identify these distractors.

Questioning the Questions

The first step in identifying distractor answers is to understand exactly what the question is asking. Read, then re-read the question, asking yourself, "What is this question actually asking?"

Keep in Mind!

1) The Question itself may give you a **keyword** to help you find the answer.
2) Each answer may have a **single word** that makes it right or wrong.
3) Even if an answer is correct, another **better** answer may be the right choice.

Eliminating Distractions

Steps to Distractor Elimination:

1) Read the question carefully. Try to answer it in your head before looking at the answers.

2) Read the answers. Eliminate any answers you **know** are incorrect.

3) From the remaining answers, see if the question has a **clue** to help you eliminate incorrect answers or select the correct one.

4) Rank each remaining answer based on how well it answers the question. Pick the highest ranked one.

5) If you have to guess, choose the one that seems or feels best.

Written composition: Expository

Read the information in the box below.

> "If you can fill the unforgiving minute
>
> With sixty seconds' worth of distance run,
>
> Yours is the Earth and everything that's in it"
>
> ~ Rudyard Kipling

You can never move forward if your eyes are fixed on the past. Think carefully about this statement.

Write an essay explaining the importance of forward thinking.

Be sure to –

- Clearly state your <u>Thesis</u>
- <u>Organize</u> and <u>Develop</u> your <u>Ideas</u> effectively
- <u>Choose</u> your <u>Words</u> carefully
- <u>Edit</u> your writing for <u>Grammar,</u> <u>Mechanics</u> and <u>Spelling</u>

Helpful Hint: Use this sheet for notes and to gather your thoughts before starting the essay – just like you should on the STAAR.

DO NOT WRITE OUTSIDE THE BOX PROVIDED

Expository Essay

	Yes	No	
Is there a clear thesis that restates and specifically addresses the prompt?	☐	☐	→ 1
		↓	
Does the writer attempt to develop ideas? (Avoids repetition)	☐	☐	→ 1
		↓	
Writing errors do not severely impact the fluency of the essay.	☐	☐	→ 1
		↓	
Ideas are well connected and address the writer's topic.	☐	☐	→ 2
		↓	
Writer supports thesis with <u>specific</u> persuasive evidence <u>*THROUGHOUT*</u>.	☐	☐	→ 2
		↓	
Can the essay be read smoothly?	☐	☐	→ 2
		↓	
Writer provides unique viewpoints/reflections.	☐	☐	→ 3
		↓	
Writer uses strong diction to promote purpose.	☐	☐	→ 3
		↓	
Sentence variety is used effectively.	☐	☐	→ 3
		↓	
		4	

Defining the Genre and Genre Characteristics:

Drama can be a very fun genre due to its focus on Dialogue and Action. The written form of a drama is called a script. It consists of characters, stage directions, dialogue and scenes that change with each setting. Dialogue in scripts is intended to be spoken aloud with inflection and emotion. It's all about acting it out (**Think:** Movies, TV Shows, Plays and Musicals).

Drama is a creative work that is composed to be performed in front of an audience.

You know a story is a Drama if it:

- Is separated into one or more Acts with smaller Scenes
- Is (mainly) either a comedy (has a happy ending) or a tragedy (ends with a loss)
- Has a story that is told through conversations between characters and contains stage directions
- Heavily relies on the audience's ability to infer characters' traits through indirect characterization
- Can be performed live or recorded
- Has theatrical elements (**Think:** Star-crossed love affair, Exaggerated reactions to situations, etc.) that can be portrayed by actors

Examples of Dramas for High School Readers:

- *Romeo and Juliet* by William Shakespeare
- *The Crucible* by Arthur Miller
- *Our Town* by Thornton Wilder
- *A Raisin in the Sun* by Lorraine Hansberry
- *Arsenic and Old Lace* by Joseph Kesselring
- *The Glass Menagerie* by Tennessee Williams
- *The Importance of Being Earnest* by Oscar Wilde

Doodles & Notes Page
Use and Enjoy

TARGETED Terminology — Drama

- **Playwright** – The author of a drama.

- **Act** – A major division of a dramatic work.

- **Scene** – A subdivision of an Act within a dramatic work at a specific setting with specific characters.

- **Stage directions** – Markers on a dramatic work that indicate actions within a scene, relevant character movements, actions and emotions.

- **Dialogue** – Conversations amongst characters.

- **Monologue** – An extended speech by one character where the character speaks to other characters.

- **Soliloquies** – An extended speech by one character where the character speaks their own thoughts aloud.

- **Asides** – When the character directly addresses the audience (**Think:** Deadpool breaking the 4th wall).

- **Parody** – A creative work made to imitate a subject (**Think:** Caricature of a subject).

- **Satire** – The use of humor and ridicule to illuminate a social issue (**Think:** Political cartoons).

Doodles & Notes Page
Use and Enjoy

Mini lesson to ensure success in the Drama genre

DRAMATIC LANGUAGE

Shakespeare's writing is arguably the most influential on English literature. However, it can be hard to understand. But, with a little practice, you can be an expert!

TRANSLATING SHAKESPEARE TO MODERN ENGLISH

Reading Shakespeare can be a lot of fun with the right tools!

THOU/THEE = YOU

THY/THINE = YOUR

ANON = SOON

HATH = HAVE

ART = ARE

DOST = DOES

TIS = IT IS

TWAS = IT WAS

AY = YES

HENCE = FROM HERE

PRAY/PRITHEE = ASK

HARK = LISTEN

Practice: Shakespearean Insults

Directions: Begin your insult with "thou" and then choose a word from each column. Use a dictionary to write the modern translation of your insult beside it!

Column 1	Column 2	Column 3
artless	beef-witted	barnacle
bootless	clapper-clawed	bugbear
currish	dizzy-eyed	canker-blossom
froward	elf-skinned	clotpole
infectious	half-faced	gudgeon
mammering	idle-headed	hedge-pig
reeky	milk-livered	lout
spleeny	sheep-biting	mammet
tottering	swag-bellied	pigeon-egg
venomed	weather-bitten	whey-face

1 <u>Thou artless folly fallen gudgeon!</u> = <u>You naïve, foolish goblin!</u>

2 _____ = _____

3 _____ = _____

Doodles & Notes Page
Use and Enjoy

Read the selection, then choose and circle the best answer to each question.

from

Romeo and Juliet
Act III : Scene 1

By William Shakespeare

(1) (Enter ROMEO)

TYBALT

Well, peace be with you, sir: here comes my man.

MERCUTIO

(5) But I'll be hanged, sir, if he wear your livery:

Marry, go before to field, he'll be your follower;

Your worship in that sense may call him 'man.'

TYBALT

Romeo, the hate I bear thee can afford no better term than this,--thou art a

(10) villain.

ROMEO

Tybalt, the reason that I have to love thee doth much excuse the appertaining

rage to such a greeting: villain am I none; therefore farewell; I see thou know'st

me not.

(15) TYBALT

Boy, this shall not excuse the injuries that thou hast done me; therefore turn and

draw.

ROMEO

(20)

I do protest, I never injured thee, but love thee better than thou canst devise, till

thou shalt know the reason of my love: and so, good Capulet,--which name I

tender as dearly as my own,--be satisfied.

MERCUTIO

O calm, dishonourable, vile submission!

Alla stoccata carries it away.

(25)   (Draws)

Tybalt, you rat-catcher, will you walk?

TYBALT

What wouldst thou have with me?

MERCUTIO

(30)

Good king of cats, nothing but one of your nine lives; that I mean to make bold

withal, and as you shall use me hereafter, drybeat the rest of the eight.

Will you pluck your sword out of his scabbard by the ears?

Make haste, lest mine be about your ears ere it be out.

TYBALT

(35)   I am for you.

(Drawing)

ROMEO

Gentle Mercutio, put thy rapier up.

MERCUTIO

(40)   Come, sir, your passado.

(They fight)

ROMEO

Draw, Benvolio; beat down their weapons.

Gentlemen, for shame, forbear this outrage!

(45)   Tybalt, Mercutio, the prince expressly hath forbidden bandying in Verona

streets: hold, Tybalt!

Good Mercutio!

(TYBALT under ROMEO's arm stabs MERCUTIO, and flies with his followers)

MERCUTIO

(50)   I am hurt.

A plague o' both your houses! I am sped.

Is he gone, and hath nothing?

BENVOLIO

What, art thou hurt?

(55)   MERCUTIO

Ay, ay, a scratch, a scratch; marry, 'tis enough.

Where is my page? Go, villain, fetch a surgeon.

(Exit Page)

ROMEO

(60)   Courage, man; the hurt cannot be much.

MERCUTIO

No, 'tis not so deep as a well, nor so wide as a church-door; but 'tis enough, 'twill

serve: ask for me to-morrow, and you shall find me a grave man.

I am peppered, I warrant, for this world.

(65)   A plague o' both your houses!

'Zounds, a dog, a rat, a mouse, a cat, to scratch a man to death!

A braggart, a rogue, a villain, that fights by the book of arithmetic!

Why the devil came you between us?

I was hurt under your arm.

(70)   ROMEO

I thought all for the best.

MERCUTIO

Help me into some house, Benvolio, or I shall faint.

A plague o' both your houses!

(75)   They have made worms' meat of me: I have it, and soundly too: your houses!

(Exeunt MERCUTIO and BENVOLIO)

ROMEO

This gentleman, the prince's near ally, my very friend, hath got his mortal hurt in

my behalf; my reputation stain'd with Tybalt's slander,--Tybalt, that an hour hath

(80)   been my kinsman!

O sweet Juliet, thy beauty hath made me effeminate and in my temper soften'd

valour's steel!

(Re-enter BENVOLIO)

BENVOLIO

(85)   O Romeo, Romeo, brave Mercutio's dead!

That gallant spirit hath aspired the clouds, which too untimely here did scorn the earth.

ROMEO

This day's black fate on more days doth depend; this but begins the woe, others

(90)   must end.

Juliet's Balcony in Verona

Drama: Questions Part 1 – from *Romeo and Juliet*

1 What is meant by "house" in Mercutio's words "A plague o' both your houses!"?

   A   Dwelling

   B   Extended family

   C   Government building

   D   Political party

E1.7(A)

2 Tybalt's grudge against Romeo resulted in Mercutio's demise. What is the author's intended message concerning these events?

   F   Danger can come even when least expected

   G   The impact of hatred spreads beyond the concerned parties

   H   Conflict is often unjustified and one-sided

   J   It is better to mediate a conflict than to escalate it

E1.6(A)

3 Mercutio and Tybalt are Character Foils. How are these two individuals best characterized?

   A   Tybalt and Mercutio are hot-headed

   B   Tybalt and Mercutio are light-hearted

   C   Tybalt is light-hearted; Mercutio is hot-headed

   D   Tybalt is hot-headed; Mercutio is light-hearted

E1.6(B)

4 What dramatic convention below most closely identifies the technique Shakespeare uses in Lines 61 – 69?

F   Monologue

G   Aside

H   Dramatic Irony

J   Soliloquy

E1.7(C)

5 What is the significance of the color 'black', modifying fate on Line 89?

A   Evokes sensory details of the settings

B   It is an omen of terrible events to come

C   It is a message of fate being evil

D   It describes Romeo's emotional state

E1.8(D)

> Will you pluck your sword out of his scabbard by the ears?

6 Shakespeare uses what literary device in this quotation?

F   Simile

G   Personification

H   Allusion

J   Hyperbole

E1.8(E)

7 What does Mercutio mean by "a grave man" in Line 63?

   A A sad man

   B A stoic man

   C An angry man

   D A dead man

E1.2(B)

8 Using contextual clues, what is a synonym for "bandying" in Line 45.

   F Loitering

   G Arguing

   H Fighting

   J Gambling

E1.2(C)

MINDFUL *moment*

"The mind is not a vessel to be filled but a fire to be kindled"
~ Plutarch

Mindful coloring is focusing on the present moment as you color. Don't worry about the final product or any small errors. Rather, choose colors that fit your mood and focus your mind on your hands and the colors as you work.

Yellow - Joy

Red - Passion

Green - Envy

Blue - Tranquil

Purple - Ambitious

Pink - Love

Orange - Confident

Brown - Grounded

Gold - Intellectual

Silver - Glamorous

White - Empty

Gray - Secure

Black - Gloomy

Doodles & Notes Page
Use and Enjoy

Read the selection, then choose and circle the best answer to each question.

From

He Said, She Said

By Alice Gerstenberg

(1)   DIANA: Mrs. Packard said that Enid said that you said you were in love with me or something like that--and that Enid hates me--

FELIX: That's not true, I know she likes you--

DIANA: But Mrs. Packard wouldn't dare say anything--

(5)   FELIX: She said Enid hates you--

DIANA: Perhaps Enid does--perhaps she is jealous over nothing at all--perhaps she has been imagining things--perhaps she does hate me--perhaps she too has been saying things--making it seem as if--

[She stops as Enid enters followed by Mrs. Packard center.]

(10)   ENID: Diana, Mrs. Packard says you insulted her and that she feels she cannot stay for dinner--

DIANA: I apologized to Mrs. Packard but she would not accept my--

MRS. PACKARD: Ah, you do admit you insulted me--

DIANA: Only after you insulted me!

103

(15)   MRS. PACKARD: You hear, Mrs. Haldeman? It is just as I said, she accused me of insulting her when I was trying only to be kind and giver her a little motherly advice--

DIANA: Mrs. Packard took it upon herself to repeat some things that people are saying--things that are manifestly untrue--

(20)   ENID: Whether they are true or not--it is highly unpleasant for me to have this altercation in my house--

DIANA: I can tell by your voice that you are willing to believe that woman--

MRS. PACKARD: Mrs. Haldeman, I resent being called that woman--

DIANA: I don't care what you resent--you've come in and spoilt a beautiful
(25)   friendship I've had all my life and I don't care what I call you--

ENID: But in my house--my guests--

DIANA: Don't worry--I shall not be your guest another moment--I'm going--(Starts.)

ENID: No, Diana, I can't let you leave in--anger.

(30)   DIANA: But I do--I leave with my heart black against you for listening to what she said--

MRS. PACKARD: What did I say?

104

DIANA: You said that Felix and I were in love with each other and you insinuated that--

(35)   MRS. PACKARD: I never said such a thing in all my life!

DIANA: Mrs. Packard! Why just a few moments ago in this very room you--

MRS. PACKARD: I never said such a thing in all my life!

DIANA: Can you look me straight in the eyes and tell me you never said it?

MRS. PACKARD: I never said it! never, never, never!

(40)   DIANA: Didn't you tell me that you have eyes and ears and that you can see and hear--and that everybody was saying--

MRS. PACKARD: But what everybody else says isn't what I say!

DIANA: Didn't you tell me that Felix was in love with me--

MRS. PACKARD: I didn't know that! She told me that! (Turns to Enid.)

(45)   ENID: I never told you that!

MRS. PACKARD: Why, my dear, you did! In this very room, a few moments ago--

ENID: I never said such a thing in all my life--and how can you imagine-

MRS. PACKARD: I imagine nothing! I know what I see and what I hear and you certainly told me that you ought to know all I had heard so you could protect yourself. So I told you in a friendly way, trying to be a help and there we are.

(50)

DIANA: (Bitterly) Yes, where are we?

MRS. PACKARD: You have no one to blame but yourself.

DIANA: We have no one to blame but you--

ENID: MRS. PACKARD, I didn't know I had to protect myself--until you insinuated-

(55)

MRS. PACKARD: Why, it was you yourself who said that he wanted to marry her--

ENID: I said nothing of the sort. I said that he said--

[All women turn simultaneously upon Felix who up to this time has refrained from meddling in the quarrel. He is confused by this sudden demand upon him and answers foolishly.]

(60)

FELIX: I don't know what you're talking about.

Drama: Questions Part 2 – from *He Said, She Said*

1 Using the dialogue between the three women, the author makes a critique on what human tendency?

   A Marriage

   B Gossip

   C Jealousy

   D Socializing

E1.6(A)

2 The final line of the passage characterizes Felix as –

   F dense

   G earnest

   H oblivious

   J inconsiderate

E1.6(B)

3 How does the setting impact the overall story?

   A It shows the reader Felix's background story

   B It allowed for Diana and Enid to share information

   C It produces a mood of light-hearted banter

   D It enabled the social interaction that resulted in a conflict

E1.6(D)

4 What do the dashes on the ends of lines throughout the passage indicate?

   F Interruptions

   G Trailing off of the speaker's words

   H Intentional syntax by the author

   J Emotional pauses

E1.7(C)

---

5 The lines inside of [brackets] are called –

   A scenes

   B acts

   C stage directions

   D dialogue

E1.7

---

6 The parallel construction used in Lines 6 – 8 indicates that Diana may be feeling –

   F disdain

   G paranoid

   H infatuation

   J relieved

E1.6

108

Testing TIPS

Using the Dictionary for Success

When taking the English I STAAR Test, you are given the option to use a dictionary. Utilizing this resource is essential for success on the exam.

What Can I Find?

You can find the correct spelling of words, definitions and synonyms. You can also find contextual information and the words' parts of speech.

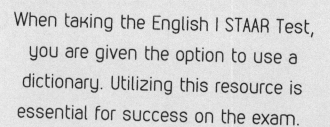

Using the Dictionary

1. Words are alphabetized so flip to the first letter of the word you are looking for, and then look at the second letter and so forth

2. You may have to scan several pages but the word **WILL** be in there

3. Some words have several meanings. Choose the definition that fits your purpose

Doodles & Notes Page
Use and Enjoy

Written composition: Expository

Read the information in the box below.

> TYBALT
>
> "What, drawn, and talk of peace? I hate the
>
> word. As I hate hell, all Montagues, and
>
> thee."
>
> ~ William Shakespeare

Do you think our words can have a huge impact on others? Think carefully about this question.

Write an essay about a time in your life when your words made a difference.

Be sure to –

- Clearly state your <u>Thesis</u>
- <u>Organize</u> and <u>Develop</u> your <u>Ideas</u> effectively
- <u>Choose</u> your <u>Words</u> carefully
- <u>Edit</u> your writing for <u>Grammar, Mechanics</u> and <u>Spelling</u>

DO NOT WRITE OUTSIDE THE BOX PROVIDED

Expository Essay

	YES	NO	
IS THERE A CLEAR THESIS THAT RESTATES AND SPECIFICALLY ADDRESSES THE PROMPT?	☐	☐ → 1
↓
DOES THE WRITER ATTEMPT TO DEVELOP IDEAS? (AVOIDS REPETITION)	☐	☐ → 1
↓
WRITING ERRORS DO NOT SEVERELY IMPACT THE FLUENCY OF THE ESSAY.	☐	☐ → 1
↓
IDEAS ARE WELL CONNECTED AND ADDRESS THE WRITER'S TOPIC.	☐	☐ → 2
↓
WRITER SUPPORTS THESIS WITH <u>SPECIFIC</u> PERSUASIVE EVIDENCE <u>*THROUGHOUT*</u>.	☐	☐ → 2
↓
CAN THE ESSAY BE READ SMOOTHLY?	☐	☐ → 2
↓
WRITER PROVIDES UNIQUE VIEWPOINTS/REFLECTIONS.	☐	☐ → 3
↓
WRITER USES STRONG DICTION TO PROMOTE PURPOSE.	☐	☐ → 3
↓
SENTENCE VARIETY IS USED EFFECTIVELY.	☐	☐ → 3
↓
4

Informational TEXTS

Defining the Genre and Genre Characteristics:

Just the facts, Jack. Informational texts are based on reality. They can be a life story, an article about tsunamis, a recipe for homemade brownies, an Algebra formula or even your history textbook. What remains the same across all the types of informational works is they are grounded in truth.

Informational texts are any unbiased work written with the purpose of informing the reader about some facet of the world.

You know a text is Informational if it:

- Includes facts (is not based solely on the author's opinions)
- Has text features such as a table of contents, a glossary, or pictures with captions
- Can be found in sources such as guidebooks, magazines, textbooks or instruction manuals
- Is structured and concise with an easy-to-read layout
- Uses clear, unambiguous language to easily convey the information
- Uses evidence, data, studies, and other reliable information

Examples of Informational works:

- A research article on the advancement of alternate energies
- A report on a current event
- A Biology teacher's printed lecture on Mitosis
- A statistic outlining the adverse effects of smoking
- A map of the United States
- A chart comparing Apple to Samsung features

Doodles & Notes Page
Use and Enjoy

- **Graphic Feature** – A visual representation of what is presented in the text to support the information.

- **Print Feature** – Used to signal when a word or idea is important (**Think:** Captions; Italics; Bold print; Titles).

- **Text Structure** (Also known as Organizational Patterns) - How the information is organized.

  o **Sequence and Order** – Presented in a chronological sequence from beginning to end (**Think:** Timelines; often history lessons.)

  o **Cause and Effect** – Identifies events, and the reasons for those events.

  o **Problem and Solution** – Provides an issue and one or more remedies to solve it.

  o **Compare and Contrast** – Author describes similarities and differences of two or more subjects (**Think:** iPhone vs Samsung reviews.)

  o **Description** – Author shares the Who, What, When, Where, Why and How of a topic.

  o **Proposition and Support** – Provides arguments (and any counter arguments) to support a given thesis statement

- **Thesis** – The main idea of the text. This is the most important sentence of an essay as it conveys the primary purpose of the writing.

- **Details** – Increases the reader's understanding through further explanation of the topic.

- **Evidence** – Facts that support the thesis statement and the author's claims.

- **Opinion** – A belief of the author's that cannot currently be proven and is not wholly based on facts.

- **Contradictory** – Evidence or details that are inconsistent with, or oppose, other statements within the same work.

- **Explanatory Essay** – Requires a logical description of a point of view, situation, issue, etc.

- **Personal Essay** – Draws on the writer's life experiences and is told from a first-person perspective.
- **Reports** – A well-researched and organized document given on a particular topic, usually as the result of a person or organization's interest or responsibility.
- **Summary** – Brief synopsis of the main points of a work.

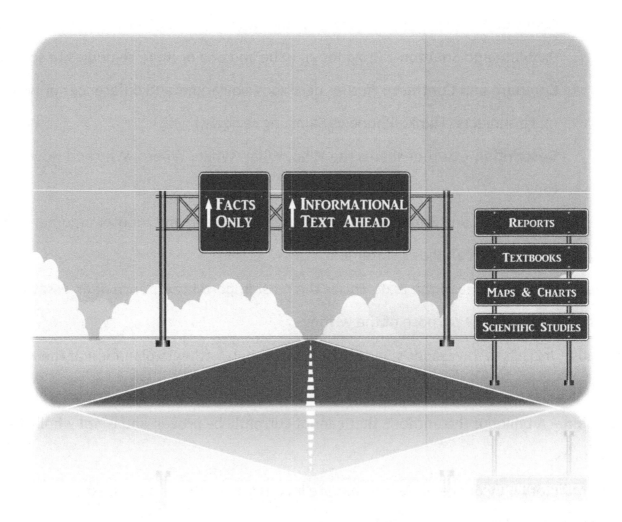

TEXT STRUCTURES

Just like with buildings, writing cannot stand without structure. Especially with informational texts, authors use text structures to organize their writing and content.

INFORMATIONAL TEXT STRUCTURES

See the various structures with their definitions and graphic organizers:

DESCRIPTION
Describes the characteristics of a topic

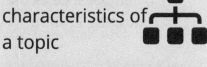

ORDER & SEQUENCE
Events/steps told in a specific order

COMPARE & CONTRAST
Compares how things are the same/differ

CAUSE & EFFECT
The reasons for and results of a situation

PROBLEM & SOLUTION
Possible remedies for a specific issue

Practice: Text Structure Scrambler

Directions: Draw a line connecting each text structure with its corresponding work

ORDER & SEQUENCE	Essay on the politics in Ancient Greece vs the Roman Empire
CAUSE & EFFECT	Diagram of the anatomy of a honey bee
DESCRIPTION	Proposal on the steps needed to clean up a polluted lake
PROBLEM & SOLUTION	Report on the events of the recent election in chronological order
COMPARE & CONTRAST	Article on the aftermath of WWII on Germany

TEXT STRUCTURES

Just like with buildings, writing cannot stand without structure. Especially with informational texts, authors use text structures to organize their writing and content.

INFORMATIONAL TEXT STRUCTURES

See the various structures with their definitions and graphic organizers:

DESCRIPTION
Describes the characteristics of a topic

ORDER & SEQUENCE
Events/steps told in a specific order

1 ___
2 ___
3 ___

COMPARE & CONTRAST
Compares how things are the same/differ

CAUSE & EFFECT
The reasons for and results of a situation

PROBLEM & SOLUTION
Possible remedies for a specific issue

Practice: Text Structure Scrambler

** SOLUTION **

ORDER & SEQUENCE	Essay on the politics in Ancient Greece vs the Roman Empire
CAUSE & EFFECT	Diagram of the anatomy of a honey bee
DESCRIPTION	Proposal on the steps needed to clean up a polluted lake
PROBLEM & SOLUTION	Report on the events of the recent election in chronological order
COMPARE & CONTRAST	Article on the aftermath of WWII on Germany

Read the selection, then choose and circle the best answer to each question.

from

The Pirates' Who's Who

By Phillip Gosse

(1) Roberts's speech to his fellow-pirates was short but to the point, saying "that since he had dipped his hands in muddy water, and must be a pirate, it was better being a commander than a common man," not perhaps a graceful nor grateful way of expressing his thanks, but one which was no doubt understood by his audience.

(2) Roberts began his career in a bright manner, for to revenge the perfectly justifiable death of their late captain he seized and razed the fort, bombarded the town, and setting on fire two Portuguese ships so as to act as torches, sailed away the same night. (3) Sailing to Brazil they found in the Bay of Bahia a fleet of forty-two Portuguese ships ready laden and on the point of leaving for Lisbon, and Roberts, with the most astounding boldness, sailed right in amongst them until he found the deepest laden, which he attacked and boarded, although his was a much smaller ship. (4) He sailed away with his prize from the harbor. (5) This prize, amongst the merchandise, contained 40,000 Moidors and a cross of diamonds designed for the King of Portugal.

(6) He then took a Dutch ship, and two days later an English one, and sailed back to Brazil, refitting and cleaning at the Island of Ferdinando.

(7) In a work such as this is, it is impossible to recount all, or even a few, of the daring adventures, or the piratical ups and downs of one pirate. (8) Roberts sailed to the West Indies devastating the commerce of Jamaica and Barbados. (9) When things grew too hot there, he went north to Newfoundland, and played the very devil with the English and French fishing fleets and settlements.

(10) His first ship he called the *Fortune*, his next, a bigger ship, the *Royal Fortune*, another the *Good Fortune*.

(11) On two occasions Roberts had been very roughly handled, once by a ship from Barbados and once by the inhabitants of Martinique, so when he designed his new flag, he portrayed on it a huge figure of himself standing sword in hand upon two skulls, and under these were the letters A.B.H. and A.M.H., signifying a Barbadian's and a Martinican's head.

(12) In April, 1721, Roberts was back again on the Guinea Coast, burning and plundering. (13) Amongst the prisoners he took out of one of his prizes was a clergyman. (14) The captain dearly wished to have a chaplain on board his ship to administer to the spiritual welfare of his crew, and tried all he could to persuade the parson to sign on, promising him that his only duties should be to say prayers and make punch. (15) But the prelate begged to be excused, and was at length allowed to go with all his belongings, except three prayer-books and a corkscrew—articles which were sorely needed aboard the *Royal Fortune*.

(16) The end of Roberts's career was now in sight. (17) A King's ship, the *Swallow* (Captain Chaloner Ogle), discovered Roberts's ships at Parrot Island, and, pretending to fly from them, was followed out to sea by one of the pirates. (18) A fight took place, and after two hours the pirates struck, flinging overboard their black flag "that it might not rise in Judgement over them." (19) The *Swallow* returned in a few days to Parrot Island to look for Roberts in the *Royal Fortune*. (20) Roberts being at breakfast, enjoying a savory dish of Solomon Gundy, was informed of the approach of the ship, but refused to take any notice of it. (21) At last, thoroughly alarmed, he cut his cables and sailed out, but most of his crew being drunk, even at this early hour, the pirates did not make as good a resistance as if they had been sober. (22) Early in the engagement Roberts was hit in the throat by a grape-shot and killed; this being on February 10th, 1722. (23) His body, fully dressed, with his arms and ornaments, was thrown overboard according to his repeated request made during his lifetime. (24) Thus the arch-pirate died, as he always said he wished to die, fighting. (25) His motto had always been "A short life and a merry one." (26) One good word can be said for Roberts, that he never forced a man to become a pirate against his wish.

Informational: Questions Part 1 – from *The Pirates' Who's Who*

1 Clues to the organizational pattern used in this passage and its structure include –

   A the words: ***Roberts began*** (line 2), ***He then*** (line 6) and ***The end*** (line 16) creating a Sequence and Order text structure

   B the words: ***Roberts's speech*** (line 1), ***to revenge*** (line 2) and ***April, 1721*** (line 12) creating a Description text structure

   C the words: ***justifiable death*** (line 2), ***devastating the*** (line 8) and ***was hit*** (line 22) creating a Cause and Effect text structure

   D the words: ***since he*** (line 1), ***went north*** (line 9) and ***thrown overboard*** (line 23) creating a Problem and Solution text structure

E1.8(B)

2 What did the author mean when he wrote, "played the very devil" in line 9?

   F Roberts was devil-like in his appearance

   G The English and French fishing fleets and settlements were superstitious of the pirates

   H He devastated the English and French fishing fleets and settlements

   J Roberts used his reputation to convince the English and French fishing fleets and settlements he was a devil

E1.8(D)

3 This passage is an Informational Text characterized by all of the following except -

   A it includes facts, and is not based in the author's opinions

   B it is based on reality with fabricated characters, situations or settings

   C it is structured and concise with an easy-to-read layout

   D it uses clear, unambiguous language to easily convey the information

E1.7(D)

4 One can infer from this selection that the author's purpose for writing *The Pirates' Who's Who* was to –

    F inform

    G persuade

    H entertain

    J confirm

E1.8

---

5 What point of view does the author use in this passage from *The Pirates' Who's Who*?

    A 1st Person

    B 2nd Person

    C 3rd Person-omniscient

    D 3rd Person-limited

E1.8

---

6 The author did not create a formal thesis for this passage. Which of the following sentences would best describe the overall theme to provide a thesis?

    F Roberts was a pirate in the 1700's who plundered towns, ships and settlements until he died.

    G Roberts, a notorious pirate in the 1700's, was killed during a battle at Parrot Island.

    H Roberts plundered and fought throughout his pirating career, ultimately dying as he lived, fighting.

    J Roberts, a pirate who stole many ships and plundered many forts and settlements, died during a battle at Parrot Island.

E1.7(D)(i)

7 Which of the following sentences does not support the author's main idea in this passage?

   A Sentence 22

   B Sentence 16

   C Sentence 12

   D Sentence 1

E1.7(D)(i)

---

8 Which of the following sentences, based on the overall theme of the message, provides the best conclusion?

   F Sentence 23

   G Sentence 24

   H Sentence 25

   J Sentence 26

E1.7(D)(i)

Doodles & Notes Page
Use and Enjoy

MINDFUL *moment*

Grounding is a calming technique that connects you with the present by exploring the five senses. Sitting or standing, take a deep breath in, and complete the following questions.

1 5 things you can see

2 4 things you can touch

3 3 things you can hear

4 2 things you can smell

5 1 thing you can taste

Read the selection, then choose and circle the best answer to each question.

A BRIEF HISTORY OF NASA

OCTOBER 1, 1958

NASA opened for business and began Project Mercury, its first project, shortly after.

JULY 20, 1969

Neil Armstrong and Buzz Aldrin became the first humans to walk on the moon.

JUNE 18, 1983

Sally Ride became the first American woman in space.

JANUARY 28, 1986

The space shuttle Challenger exploded shortly after its launch.

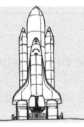

APRIL 25, 1990

The Hubble space telescope was deployed and has since changed how we view the universe.

JANUARY 22, 2010

The first tweet was sent from space by astronaut T.J. Creamer.

SOURCE: WWW.NASA.GOV

1 What evidence within the graphic demonstrates a Sequence and Order structure?

    A Evolution of technology

    B Women and tweets in space

    C Use of dates

    D The graphic is not in a Sequence and Order structure

E1.7(D)

2 What can we infer about the author's message from the graphic?

    F Space has changed a lot since NASA started

    G NASA accomplished much and had some challenges in its first half century

    H In 52 years, NASA went from being created to sending tweets in space

    J Sally Ride was the first woman in space

E1.8(A)

3 How does the organizational pattern of this graphic support its message?

    A Provides a series of events to give a glimpse of NASA's failures

    B Provides a series of events to give a glimpse at NASA's accomplishments

    C Provides a series of events to give a glimpse at NASA's historic moments

    D Provides a series of events to give a glimpse of NASA's important people

E1.7(D)(ii)

4 How do the print features of the graphic enhance its effectiveness?

F Provide concrete examples of NASA's past events

G Provide abstract examples of NASA's past events

H Provide concrete examples of NASA's ambitions

J Provide abstract examples of NASA's ambitions

E1.8(C)

5 How do the graphic features of this graphic enhance its effectiveness?

A Provide an accurate rendering of described events to increase reader visualization

B Provide a correlated rendering of described events to increase reader visualization

C Demonstrate effective use of tone to enhance the author's message

D Demonstrate effective use of mood to enhance the author's message

E1.8(C)

6 Which of the events listed on the graphic most likely had the greatest impact on NASA?

F April 25, 1990

G January 28, 1986

H July 20, 1969

J October 1, 1958

E1.4

Doodles & Notes Page
Use and Enjoy

Testing TIPS
Close Reading and Following Directions

Close reading is analyzing a text and taking notes as you read for important details, organizational patterns, author's craft, themes, etc. You are allowed to take notes on the testing booklet, use this to fully immerse yourself in the reading sections.

Following Directions

Do **NOT** skim the questions! You could miss a single word that completely changes your understanding of the question resulting in an incorrect answer.

How to Close Read

1. Read the questions before the passage to understand the reading focus
2. Read the passage at least twice.
3. Circle any words that you do not know to look up in the dictionary
4. Underline main ideas and important concepts
5. Paraphrase controlling statements in the margins

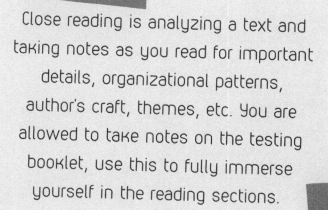

9 Which of the following sentences contains a run-on sentence caused by a comma splice?

A Sentence 11

B Sentence 6

C Sentence 10

D Sentence 20

Note: If you miss the key phrase, "Comma Splice" you may choose the wrong answer.

Doodles & Notes Page
Use and Enjoy

Written composition: Expository

Read the information in the box below.

> "One day, technology will replace man as the primary worker on the globe. This is happening. This is inevitable."
>
> ~ Anonymous

What do you think is the most important modern technology? Think carefully about this question.

Write an essay about a new technology that you believe will impact the future the most.

Be sure to –

- Clearly state your Thesis
- Organize and Develop your Ideas effectively
- Choose your Words carefully
- Edit your writing for Grammar, Mechanics and Spelling

Helpful Hint: Use this sheet for notes and to gather your thoughts before starting the essay – just like you should on the STAAR.

STAAR CHECKLIST

Expository Essay

	Yes	No	
Is there a clear thesis that restates and specifically addresses the prompt?	☐	☐	→ 1
↓			
Does the writer attempt to develop ideas? (Avoids repetition)	☐	☐	→ 1
↓			
Writing errors do not severely impact the fluency of the essay.	☐	☐	→ 1
↓			
Ideas are well connected and address the writer's topic.	☐	☐	→ 2
↓			
Writer supports thesis with SPECIFIC persuasive evidence THROUGHOUT.	☐	☐	→ 2
↓			
Can the essay be read smoothly?	☐	☐	→ 2
↓			
Writer provides unique viewpoints/reflections.	☐	☐	→ 3
↓			
Writer uses strong diction to promote purpose.	☐	☐	→ 3
↓			
Sentence variety is used effectively.	☐	☐	→ 3
↓			
4			

138

Argumentative Texts

Defining the Genre and Genre Characteristics:

Do you want to learn how to convince your parents to give you a later curfew? Then you should study Rhetorical Devices. The art of the argumentative genre is using strategies to effectively communicate a rational, non-emotional belief in an attempt to sway the audience's opinion. After studying this unit, you may find that your ability to persuade others in a logical, concise and well-developed manner has greatly improved.

Argumentative Text contains any work in which the purpose is to sway the opinion of the audience to the opinion of the author or speaker.

You know a work is Argumentative if it:

- Is well researched, accurate and detailed
- Contains one or more arguments and counterarguments, all to funnel opinion to the author's claim
- Has a thesis statement that is the focus of the debate or speech
- Begins with the claim, followed by multiple clear, supporting details
- Is plainly stated (without the flowery, indirect language found in literary works)
- Often concludes with a call to action

Examples of common debate topics:

- Animal Testing
- The Death Penalty
- Gun Control
- Use of Cell Phones in Schools
- Mandated School Uniforms
- Driving Age
- Paying Student Athletes

Doodles & Notes Page
Use and Enjoy

- **Argument** – The persuasive topic that is supported with evidence (**Think:** Whether the earth is flat or round). This in not like an 'argument' you would have with a sibling.

- **Message** – What the author is trying to persuade the reader to believe.

- **Claim** – A statement made by the author that they assert is true. This claim is the core of the argument that can be disputed by others.

- **Refute** – To disprove a statement.

- **Counterargument** (also known as Rebuttal) – A response to an opposing viewpoint with the goal of refuting the argument.

- **Concession** – A strategy where the author concedes to small valid points to establish credibility and neutralize that particular argument from debate.

- **Rhetorical Device(s)** – Techniques used by an author or speaker to convey their message.

  - **Ethos** – An appeal to credibility. The author tries to establish trust with the audience through common values, their credentials, celebrity, etc. (**Think:** A cold beverage commercial using a celebrity to sell its product).

  - **Pathos** – An appeal to emotion. The author tries to inspire an emotional response within the audience (**Think:** A commercial displaying a sad puppy to get donations for an animal shelter).

  - **Logos** – An appeal to logic. The author uses facts, figures, statistics and deductive reasoning (**Think:** A Public Service Announcement using scientific studies to discourage underage drinking).

- **Significant** – Particularly important (especially with regard to the argument).

- **Sensory Images** – Author provides visual imagery to engage a reader's mind to create a mental image.

- **Current Events** – Important affairs or developments occurring in the world right now (**Think:** COVID in 2020).

- **Eyewitnesses** (also known as First-hand Accounts) – A person who has seen something happen personally (**Think:** A teller filing a police report after being held up during a bank robbery).
- **Overestimate** – Perceiving the value of a subject to be higher than reality (**Think:** A treasured ring believed to be priceless, but it is not gold and has no gemstone).
- **Underestimate** – Perceiving the value of a subject to be lower than reality (**Think:** A huge problem said to be "only a slight inconvenience" by a speaker)
- **Logical Fallacies** – Flaws in reasoning that undermine legitimate arguments (**Think:** These are false assertions and not what to do in a debate). There are many types of Logical Fallacies, below are several of them:
  - **Red Herring** – A distraction from the argument that is loosely related, but not on topic (**Think:** Quoting the number of drunk driving deaths in an argument about the health impacts of smoking).
  - **Strawman** – Attacking a simplified version of the opponent's argument (**Think:** Saying, "Those who refuse to get vaccinated, don't care about the elderly").
  - **Slippery Slope** – The author establishes a pattern (in the future) that will occur if the counter argument path is followed (**Think:** If we develop robots, then eventually no one will be employed as everyone's job is taken by robots, therefore we should not develop robots).
  - **Bandwagon** – An appeal that pressures the reader to follow popular opinions to sway the audience (**Think:** Tik Tok influencers teaching all of their followers a dance and those followers posting the same dance until it is trending).
  - **Either-Or** (also known as false dilemma) – Oversimplifying and falsely claiming that there are only two options: The argument the speaker is trying to make or a negative outcome (**Think:** We can either go out to eat or starve).
  - **Begging the Question** (also known as avoiding the question) – The author assumes the argument is true without actually proving it (**Think:** Everyone loves Nike because they are the most popular shoe company).

DEBATE ETIQUETTE

When debating a topic with another person, it is important to be courteous even while you disagree with their stance. This is how to have productive exchanges of ideas.

FORMAL DEBATE STRUCTURE

Begins with the affirmative (in favor) side and then the negative (against). The sides take turns and follow this general outline:

OPENING STATEMENT

States the topic and several arguments to back it up
+ animal testing is beneficial for creating cures for diseases and is more ethical than using human subjects.
- animal testing is a cruel and inhumane practice on species that are not necessarily biologically compatible

REBUTTAL

Defends the arguments and refutes opponents points
+ Most scientific and health specialists endorse animal testing and strive to be humane to ensure testing reliability
- Stem cell studies have shown great promise while 94% of drugs that pass animal tests fail human clinical studies

CLOSING STATEMENT

Responds to opponent's points and sums up argument
+ animal testing is highly regulated and has resulted in major advances regarding numerous diseases
- alternative testing methods are just as effective and there are more demands for cruelty free products than ever

Topic: Animal Testing

Practice: Mini Debate

Directions: choose a topic you feel strongly about and research both sides on procon.org and have a debate with yourself below!

OPENING STATEMENT

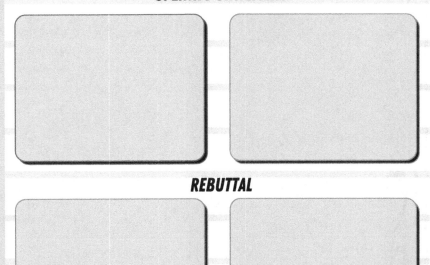

REBUTTAL

CLOSING STATEMENT

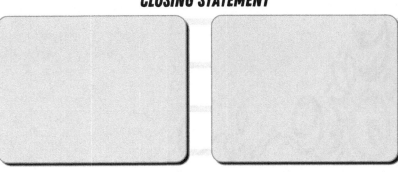

Read the selection and choose and circle the best answer to each question.

from

Inaugural Address of John F. Kennedy
January 20, 1961

By John F. Kennedy

(1) Let every nation know, whether it wishes us well or ill, that we shall pay any price, bear any burden, meet any hardship, support any friend, oppose any foe, in order to assure the survival and the success of liberty.

(2) This much we pledge--and more.

(3) To those old allies whose cultural and spiritual origins we share, we pledge the loyalty of faithful friends. (4) United, there is little we cannot do in a host of cooperative ventures. (5) Divided, there is little we can do--for we dare not meet a powerful challenge at odds and split asunder.

(6) To those new States whom we welcome to the ranks of the free, we pledge our word that one form of colonial control shall not have passed away merely to be replaced by a far more iron tyranny. (7) We shall not always expect to find them supporting our view. (8) But we shall always hope to find them strongly supporting their own freedom--and to remember that, in the past, those who foolishly sought power by riding the back of the tiger ended up inside.

(9) To those peoples in the huts and villages across the globe struggling to break the bonds of mass misery, we pledge our best efforts to help them help themselves, for whatever period is required--not because the Communists may be doing it, not because we seek their votes, but because it is right. (10) If a free society cannot help the many who are poor, it cannot save the few who are rich.

(11) To our sister republics south of our border, we offer a special pledge--to convert our good words into good deeds--in a new alliance for progress--to assist free men and free governments in casting off the chains of poverty. (12) But this peaceful revolution of hope cannot become the prey of hostile powers. (13) Let all our neighbors know that we shall join with them to oppose aggression or subversion anywhere in the Americas. (14) And let every other power know that this Hemisphere intends to remain the master of its own house.

(15) To that world assembly of sovereign states, the United Nations, our last best hope in an age where the instruments of war have far outpaced the instruments of peace, we renew our pledge of support--to prevent it from becoming merely a forum for invective--to strengthen its shield of the new and the weak--and to enlarge the area in which its writ may run.

(16) Finally, to those nations who would make themselves our adversary, we offer not a pledge but a request: that both sides begin anew the quest for peace, before the dark powers of destruction unleashed by science engulf all humanity in planned or accidental self-destruction.

(17) We dare not tempt them with weakness. (18) For only when our arms are sufficient beyond doubt can we be certain beyond doubt that they will never be employed.

(19) But neither can two great and powerful groups of nations take comfort from our present course--both sides overburdened by the cost of modern weapons, both rightly alarmed by the steady spread of the deadly atom, yet both racing to alter that uncertain balance of terror that stays the hand of mankind's final war.

(20) So let us begin anew--remembering on both sides that civility is not a sign of weakness, and sincerity is always subject to proof. (21) Let us never negotiate out of fear. (22) But let us never fear to negotiate.

(23) Let both sides explore what problems unite us instead of belaboring those problems which divide us.

(24) Let both sides, for the first time, formulate serious and precise proposals for the inspection and control of arms--and bring the absolute power to destroy other nations under the absolute control of all nations.

(25) Let both sides seek to invoke the wonders of science instead of its terrors. (26) Together let us explore the stars, conquer the deserts, eradicate disease, tap the ocean depths, and encourage the arts and commerce.

(27) Let both sides unite to heed in all corners of the earth the command of Isaiah--to "undo the heavy burdens ... and to let the oppressed go free."

(28) And if a beachhead of cooperation may push back the jungle of suspicion, let both sides join in creating a new endeavor, not a new balance of power, but a new world of law, where the strong are just and the weak secure and the peace preserved.

(29) All this will not be finished in the first 100 days. (30) Nor will it be finished in the first 1,000 days, nor in the life of this Administration, nor even perhaps in our lifetime on this planet. (31) But let us begin.

(32) In your hands, my fellow citizens, more than in mine, will rest the final success or failure of our course. (33) Since this country was founded, each generation of Americans has been summoned to give testimony to its national loyalty. (34) The graves of young Americans who answered the call to service surround the globe.

(35) Now the trumpet summons us again--not as a call to bear arms, though arms we need; not as a call to battle, though embattled we are--but a call to bear the burden of a long twilight struggle, year in and year out, "rejoicing in hope, patient in tribulation"--a struggle against the common enemies of man: tyranny, poverty, disease, and war itself.

(36) Can we forge against these enemies a grand and global alliance, North and South, East and West, that can assure a more fruitful life for all mankind? (37) Will you join in that historic effort?

(38) In the long history of the world, only a few generations have been granted the role of defending freedom in its hour of maximum danger. (39) I do not shrink from this responsibility-- I welcome it. (40) I do not believe that any of us would exchange places with any other people or any other generation. (41) The energy, the faith, the devotion which we bring to this endeavor will light our country and all who serve it--and the glow from that fire can truly light the world.

(42) And so, my fellow Americans: ask not what your country can do for you--ask what you can do for your country.

(43) My fellow citizens of the world: ask not what America will do for you, but what together we can do for the freedom of man.

(44) Finally, whether you are citizens of America or citizens of the world, ask of us the same high standards of strength and sacrifice which we ask of you. (45) With a good conscience our only sure reward, with history the final judge of our deeds, let us go forth to lead the land we love, asking His blessing and His help, but knowing that here on earth God's work must truly be our own.

Argumentative: Questions Part 1 – from "Inaugural Address of John F. Kennedy"

1 Which sentence below correctly describes the organizational pattern used by Kennedy in this speech?

   A Kennedy provided a chronological sequence to identify the ordering of his message

   B Kennedy examined the similarities and differences of nations to frame his message

   C Kennedy defined a problem and provided solutions to form his message

   D Kennedy described major components of a topic to deliver his message

1.8(B)

---

2 What did Kennedy mean by *forum for invective* in sentence 15?

   F Place where people meet to discuss inventions

   G Place where people meet to argue and criticize

   H Place where people join together for business meetings

   J Place where people join together for casual meetings

1.8(D)

---

3 Which sentence below best describes Kennedy's use of rhetorical devices in sentence 19?

   A Kennedy used Logos to appeal to the audience's logical thoughts about modern warfare

   B Kennedy used Ethos to appeal to the audience's ethical thoughts about modern warfare

   C Kennedy used Ethos to appeal to the audience's belief in his credibility about modern warfare

   D Kennedy used Pathos to appeal to the audience's emotions about modern warfare

1.8(G)

4 This speech is an Argumentative Text characterized by all of the following except -

F it includes facts, and is not based on the speaker's opinions

G it has a thesis statement that is the focus of the speech

H it concludes with a call to action

J it begins with a claim followed by multiple clear, supporting details

1.7(E)

> "And so, my fellow Americans: ask not what your country can do for you--ask what you can do for your country."

5 What was Kennedy trying to convey to the audience with this statement?

A The audience should stop asking for handouts and start working for the government

B The audience should recommit to the national loyalty described in the speech

C The audience should prepare to defend freedom at its darkest hour

D The audience should focus on making the described goals a reality

1.8(A)

---

6 Which of the following sentences best summarizes Kennedy's primary claim?

F America and its allies, when cooperating, will have amazing accomplishments and will defeat any challenge that presents itself

G Everyone should understand that America will meet any challenge to help our allies, to defeat our foes and to protect our nation's sovereignty.

H America pledges to support and defend our new allies and, even if they disagree with some of our views, hope they will agree that freedom is better than tyranny

J Everyone should believe that America, as the primary superpower of the global community, will protect and defend our borders to safeguard our freedom

1.7(E)(i)

---

7 What evidence does Kennedy provide to demonstrate he is committed to peace and cooperation among adversaries?

   A He commits to a reduction in nuclear weapons to ensure peace between nations

   B He challenges adversaries with America's strength to help prevent future violence

   C He provides alternative paths to adversaries that would lead to a common good

   D He assures all nations that he is taking steps to avoid conflicts in the world

E1.7(E)(ii)

---

8 Who was the intended audience of Kennedy's Inaugural Address?

   F American citizens

   G World citizens

   H America and its allies

   J Democratic nations around the world

E1.7(E)(iii)

---

9 Which of the following logical fallacies are present in Kennedy's speech?

   A Straw man in sentences 32 – 34

   B Either-or in sentences 9 – 10

   C Slippery Slope in sentences 29 – 31

   D Bandwagon in sentences 35 – 37

E1.8(E)

Doodles & Notes Page
Use and Enjoy

MINDFUL *moment*

"Give a man a fish, and you feed him for a day. Teach a man to fish and you feed him for a lifetime"
~ Maimonides

Only one hand appears multiple times in an odd number. Can you find it?

HELPING HANDS

MINDFUL *moment*

"Give a man a fish, and you feed him for a day. Teach a man to fish and you feed him for a lifetime"
~ Maimonides

Solution:

HELPING HANDS

154

Read the selection and choose and circle the best answer to each question.

From

The Declaration of Independence

By Thomas Jefferson (initial draft)

(1) When in the Course of human Events, it becomes necessary for one People to dissolve the Political Bands which have connected them with another, and to assume among the Powers of the Earth, the separate and equal Station to which the Laws of Nature and of Nature's God entitle them, a decent Respect to the Opinions of Mankind requires that they should declare the causes which impel them to the Separation.

(2) We hold these Truths to be self-evident, that all Men are created equal, that they are endowed by their Creator with certain unalienable Rights, that among these are Life, Liberty, and the Pursuit of Happiness—That to secure these Rights, Governments are instituted among Men, deriving their just Powers from the Consent of the Governed, that whenever any form of Government becomes destructive of these Ends, it is the Right of the People to alter or to abolish it, and to institute new Government, laying its Foundation on such Principles, and organizing its Powers in such form, as to them shall seem most likely to affect their Safety and Happiness.

(3) Prudence, indeed, will dictate that Governments long established should not be changed for light and transient Causes; and accordingly all Experience hath shewn, that Mankind are more disposed to suffer, while Evils are sufferable, than to right themselves by abolishing the forms to which they are accustomed.

(4) But when a long Train of Abuses and Usurpations, pursuing invariably the same Object, evinces a Design to reduce them under absolute Despotism, it is their Right, it is their Duty, to throw off such Government, and to provide new Guards for their future Security.

(5) Such has been the patient Sufferance of these Colonies; and such is now the Necessity which constrains them to alter their former Systems of Government.

(6) The History of the present King of Great-Britain is a History of repeated Injuries and Usurpations, all having in direct Object the Establishment of an absolute Tyranny over these States.

(7) To prove this, let Facts be submitted to a candid World.

(8) He has refused his Assent to Laws, the most wholesome and necessary for the public good.

(9) He has forbidden his Governors to pass Laws of immediate and pressing importance, unless suspended in their operation till his Assent should be obtained; and when so suspended, he has utterly neglected to attend to them.

(10) He has refused to pass other Laws for the accommodation of large districts of people, unless those people would relinquish the right of Representation in the Legislature, a right inestimable to them and formidable to tyrants only.

(11) He has called together legislative bodies at places unusual, uncomfortable, and distant from the depository of their public Records, for the sole purpose of fatiguing them into compliance with his measures.

(12) He has dissolved Representative Houses repeatedly, for opposing with manly firmness his invasions on the rights of the people.

·······

(13) In every stage of these Oppressions We have Petitioned for Redress in the most humble terms: Our repeated Petitions have been answered only by repeated injury. (14) A Prince whose character is thus marked by every act which may define a Tyrant, is unfit to be the ruler of a free people.

(15) Nor have We been wanting in attentions to our Brittish brethren. (16) We have warned them from time to time of attempts by their legislature to extend an unwarrantable jurisdiction over us. (17) We have reminded them of the circumstances of our emigration and settlement here. (18) We have appealed to their native justice and magnanimity, and we have conjured them by the ties of our common kindred to disavow these usurpations, which, would inevitably interrupt our connections and correspondence. (19) They too have been deaf to the voice of

justice and of consanguinity. (20) We must, therefore, acquiesce in the necessity, which denounces our Separation, and hold them, as we hold the rest of mankind, Enemies in War, in Peace Friends.

(21) We, therefore, the Representatives of the united States of America, in General Congress, Assembled, appealing to the Supreme Judge of the world for the rectitude of our intentions, do, in the Name, and by Authority of the good People of these Colonies, solemnly publish and declare, That these United Colonies are, and of Right ought to be Free and Independent States; that they are Absolved from all Allegiance to the British Crown, and that all political connection between them and the State of Great Britain, is and ought to be totally dissolved; and that as Free and Independent States, they have full Power to levy War, conclude Peace, contract Alliances, establish Commerce, and to do all other Acts and Things which Independent States may of right do. (22) And for the support of this Declaration, with a firm reliance on the protection of divine Providence, we mutually pledge to each other our Lives, our Fortunes and our sacred Honor.

Argumentative: Questions Part 2 – from "The Declaration of Independence"

1 Which of the following correctly describes the organizational pattern used in the Declaration of Independence passage?

   A **Proposition and Support** - because it makes a statement at the beginning and provides the reasoning to support that statement throughout the passage

   B **Compare and Contrast** – because it states what government should be and then contrasts this to the way government is under the king throughout the passage

   C **Description** – because it describes what facets of government the colonists are not satisfied with and provides details about these facets throughout the passage

   D **Chronological** – because it explains the status of the colonies and provides a chronology of the royal offenses to clarify how the colonies got to this state throughout the passage

E1.8(B)

2 What is the purpose of the capitalizations of words throughout the document within the sentences?

   F This was done because the rules for capitalization were different in 1776

   G This was done as a code to provide colonial insurgents with instructions

   H This was done as part of the writer's individual style

   J This was done to show emphasis

E1.8(D)

> "We hold these Truths to be self-evident, that all Men are created equal"

3 This quote can best be referred to as –

A an overstatement, because truths are not self-evident

B an understatement, because all men are always created equal

C an overstatement because truths are not self-evident and an understatement because all men are always created equal

D neither an overstatement nor an understatement

E1.8(G)

---

4 Based on the passage, what can we infer was the author's primary purpose for writing the Declaration of Independence?

F To initiate war with Britain and request foreign support

G To prevent war with Britain and propose a new government

H To declare war with Britain and denounce the king's actions

J To justify war with Britain and establish an independent government

E1.8(A)

---

5 Which of the following sentences best describes the author's primary claims?

A When certain unacceptable events in life take place, man must rise up against his oppressors to take back their rights and protect their freedom

B The king has betrayed his colonies by causing or allowing offenses to be perpetuated on the colonists and thus his rule of law is no longer valid

C People are all made equally and they own certain rights and have a duty to defend their rights, the rights of others and even replace governments when these rights are denied

D Rebellion is the just and noble duty of all citizens of free nations when met with oppression from outside forces and all men have a duty to protect themselves from oppressors

E1.7(E)(i)

> "The History of the present King of Great-Britain is a History of repeated Injuries and Usurpations, all having in direct Object the Establishment of an absolute Tyranny over these States."

6 What evidence does the writer present in the passage to support the opinion articulated in this quotation?

   F A statement explaining the *long Train of Abuses and Usurpations* and how these have impacted the colonies

   G A list of issues

   H A statement explaining that the colony must *acquiesce in the necessity, which denounces our Separation*

   J A list of responsibilities

E1.7(E)(ii)

7 Who is the intended audience of this passage?

   A The world

   B The colonies

   C The King of Great Britain

   D Foreign allies and supporters

E1.7(E)(iii)

8 The conclusion of the Declaration of Independence was –

   F effective because it restated the main ideas and supporting evidence in a new way

   G ineffective because it failed to restate the main ideas and supporting evidence in a new way

   H effective because it provided a resolution of resulting actions as expected based on the passage's organizational pattern

   J ineffective because it failed to provide a resolution of resulting actions as expected based on the passage's organizational pattern

E1.7(E)(i)

Testing TIPS

Developing a Growth Mindset

Having a **Growth Mindset** has shown to result in higher success, both academically and personally. In fact, a New York study in Harlem showed that teaching a class of low achieving Kindergarteners growth mindset resulted in exceptionally higher test scores.

Growth VS Fixed

It's the difference between saying, "I'll do better next time," and, "Wow, I'm so bad at this."

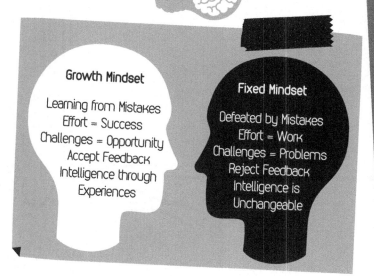

Growth Mindset

Learning from Mistakes
Effort = Success
Challenges = Opportunity
Accept Feedback
Intelligence through Experiences

Fixed Mindset

Defeated by Mistakes
Effort = Work
Challenges = Problems
Reject Feedback
Intelligence is Unchangeable

How to Speak to Yourself

1. Challenges help me grow
2. Once I've practiced enough, I will succeed
3. I love learning new things
4. Failures do not define me
5. My intelligence is not inherent; I can grow through effort
6. I have unlimited potential
7. I can do better next time
8. What can I do to improve this in the future?
9. Hard work is the path to achievement
10. Others' success is an inspiration to me

Doodles & Notes Page
Use and Enjoy

Written composition: Expository

Read the information in the box below.

> "And so, my fellow Americans: ask not what your country can do for you--ask what you can do for your country."
>
> ~ John F. Kennedy

What speech or essay have you read that impacted the way you think about something? Think carefully about this question.

Write an essay about how leaders can persuade people to make changes.

Be sure to –

- Clearly state your <u>Thesis</u>
- <u>Organize</u> and <u>Develop</u> your <u>Ideas</u> effectively
- <u>Choose</u> your <u>Words</u> carefully

<u>Edit</u> your writing for <u>Grammar</u>, <u>Mechanics</u> and <u>Spelling</u>

Helpful Hint: Use this sheet for notes and to gather your thoughts before starting the essay – just like you should on the STAAR.

DO NOT WRITE OUTSIDE THE BOX PROVIDED

STAAR CHECKLIST

Expository Essay

	YES	NO	
IS THERE A CLEAR THESIS THAT RESTATES AND SPECIFICALLY ADDRESSES THE PROMPT?	☐	☐	→ 1
		↓	
DOES THE WRITER ATTEMPT TO DEVELOP IDEAS? (AVOIDS REPETITION)	☐	☐	→ 1
		↓	
WRITING ERRORS DO NOT SEVERELY IMPACT THE FLUENCY OF THE ESSAY.	☐	☐	→ 1
		↓	
IDEAS ARE WELL CONNECTED AND ADDRESS THE WRITER'S TOPIC.	☐	☐	→ 2
		↓	
WRITER SUPPORTS THESIS WITH _SPECIFIC_ PERSUASIVE EVIDENCE _THROUGHOUT_.	☐	☐	→ 2
		↓	
CAN THE ESSAY BE READ SMOOTHLY?	☐	☐	→ 2
		↓	
WRITER PROVIDES UNIQUE VIEWPOINTS/REFLECTIONS.	☐	☐	→ 3
		↓	
WRITER USES STRONG DICTION TO PROMOTE PURPOSE.	☐	☐	→ 3
		↓	
SENTENCE VARIETY IS USED EFFECTIVELY.	☐	☐	→ 3
		↓	
		4	

Making Connections:

If you've followed this workbook in sequence, you've learned the writing foundations of editing and revision, explored the worlds of fiction, poetry and drama, examined the facts of informational texts and scrutinized the claims of argumentative texts. These genres may seem very different, and indeed they are, but by taking the plunge and diving beyond the surface of each type of writing, you can discover connections and commonality within the authors' words. Developing the ability to identify and make connections (both literary and within other fields) will help you excel in future life positions that demand this skill to be successful (**Think:** lawyer, scientist, engineer, salesperson, detective, etc.)

Making **Connections Across Genres** involves looking deeper into the overall meanings, the text structures, the authors' use of words and other similar factors that can bring seemingly unrelated texts together and form a bridge of understanding between them.

Ways to develop Connections Across Genres:

- Determine the genre of each text
- Compare and contrast:
    - *Themes, Events, Facts, Lessons, Conclusions*
    - *Organizational Patterns*
    - *Syntax, Tone, Mood, Settings, Characterizations*
    - *Authors' Purpose, Style* and *Craft*
- Develop a personal analysis of each reading
- Identify the common and contrasting ideas, styles, patterns, etc.

- **Types of connections** – There are three primary types of relationships you can make with literary connections: Text-to-Text, Text-to-Self and Text-to-World.
    - **Text-to-Text** – Connections between two or more reading passages across or within genres (**Think:** The events in the novel *Pet Sematary* to the poem "The Tell-Tale Heart".)
        - **Questions to ask yourself while reading**:
            - How are the passages similar or different?
                - **Think:** Themes, characters, authors' choice of language, mood, tone, setting, organizational patterns, etc.
            - Can you think of another story that is similar to this one?
            - How are the genre characteristics similar or different?
                - What impact does this have on the interpretation of each passage?
    - **Text-to-Self** – Personal connections you make between the reading and your own life or experiences (**Think:** A reading reminding you of a time you went fishing like in *Huckleberry Finn*)
        - **Questions to ask yourself while reading:**
            - How are you similar to the characters in the text?
            - What new information did you learn from the text?
            - How would you handle the situations presented in the text?
            - What predictions or inferences can you make on the text based on what you know?
    - **Text-to-World** – Connections between the text and world events now or in the past (**Think:** The novel *Gone with the Wind* to the Civil War.)
        - **Questions to ask yourself while reading:**
            - What connections can be made between the social issues presented in the text and the real world?
            - How do literary / rhetorical devices within the text reflect events or moral dilemmas within the real world?
            - How does the passage accurately or inaccurately reflect historic or current events?
            - How are unique cultures and beliefs represented within the text?
                - Is this representative or nonrepresentative of world cultures and beliefs?
                - Is the author using these representations to mirror or critique these concepts?

Surprise! The good news is there's no NEW readings for you to digest with the following questions. That being said, you may have to reread some passages from previous sections of the workbook to refamiliarize yourself with them to answer the following questions.

While there is no single best method for answering these type of questions (do what works best for you), one useful trick is to use a T-chart next to the answers and focus on whether or not each answer is correct for the texts presented.

Example:

To answer connections questions, try using a T-chart as follows:

- **First:** Draw a T-chart as shown beside the question.

-- The 1st column represents the 1st text

-- The 2nd column is either a second text, or the "to Self" or "to World" column.

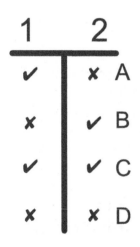

- **Next:** Focus on each answer individually, and put a ✔ if the answer applies to the 1st or 2nd (or both) columns.

- **Then:** Put an ✗ if the answer doesn't apply to the 1st or 2nd (or both) columns.

- **Finally:** The correct answer is the one where both the 1st and 2nd column have ✔s next to them.

(On the example, you would choose 'C' as correct)

Note: Don't stop at the first answer, even if it has both ✔s; This may be a trick where 'All of the Above' is correct

Mini lesson to ensure
success when making
Connections Across Genres

CONNECTED / DISCONNECTED

The process of making connections is similar no matter what media you use. Movies, for example, are simply scripts that are acted out and recorded. Likewise, what happens at someone's job is simply an informational text that hasn't been written down. Using this mindset, you can make connections across almost anything if you try hard enough.

Practice: Creating Connections

Directions: Choose 2 different movies, books, life events, etc. and make the connections in the boxes as labeled below.
This exercise works best when you use as much detail as possible!

Choice 1

Choice 2

How are the choices similar?

How are the choices different?

What life lesson can you learn from choice 1?

What world event or culture is similar to choice 2?

Doodles & Notes Page
Use and Enjoy

Reread the selection (if needed) and choose and circle the best answer to each question.

Connections Across Genres: Questions Part 1

1 All of the following statements differ between "If…" (page 71) and "Annabel Lee" (page 77) except –

  A the overall mood and tone of the poem

  B the consistency of the poetic structure

  C the narrator's dedication towards his subject

  D the message intended for the reader

E1.4(E)

2 In the "Inaugural Address of John F. Kennedy" (page 145), what global crisis can you infer most likely inspired his speech?

  F World War II

  G The Nuclear Arms Race

  H The Civil War

  J The American Revolution

E1.4(E)

3 After reading the "Inaugural Address of John F. Kennedy" (page 145) and *Frankenstein* (page 53), what can be understood about human nature?

  A The inventions of mankind can become horrible

  B Mankind is driven towards war

  C Science and technological advancements of mankind are inherently evil

  D Man should not perform genetic experimentation on humans

E1.4(H)

4 What literary element is similar between *A Christmas Carol* (page 45) and "Annabel Lee" (page 77)?

    F   A heavy use of dialogue to characterize the protagonist

    G   An extended metaphor that represents the author

    H   A strong narrative voice that critiques the protagonist's actions

    J   Sensory details that contribute to a dark and foreboding mood

E1.6

5 What lesson can be learned from reading "The Declaration of Independence" (page 155)?

    A   Government should be providing rights for its people

    B   You are responsible for defending your natural rights

    C   Problems should be solved through warfare

    D   Happiness is determined through the government's effectiveness

E1.4(E)

6 All of the following are differences between Informational and Argumentative texts except –

    F   the use of research, facts and evidence

    G   the purpose of the text is to support an author's claim

    H   the text is structured and concise with an easy-to-read layout

    J   the importance of rhetoric in conveying the message

E1.7

7 We can infer from "The Inaugural Address of John F. Kennedy" (page 145) and *Romeo and Juliet* (page 93) the importance of –

A   Tenacity

B   War

C   Peace

D   Strength

E1.8

8 What is a similar motif between both *A Brief History of NASA* (page 129) and *Frankenstein* (page 53)?

F   Historical events

G   Loss

H   World development

J   Technological advancements

E1.4(E)

Doodles & Notes Page
Use and Enjoy

MINDFUL
moment

"We can complain because rose bushes have thorns, or rejoice because thorn bushes have roses."
~ Abraham Lincoln

Find some time for meditative journaling. A list of possible journal prompts have been provided for you, but you can choose any topic you like.

Mindfulness Journal Prompts

1. **Thinking about the people in my life who care for me, what am I grateful for?**
2. **What are my most important values?**
3. **What are a few qualities I love the most about myself?**
4. **What is my ten year plan?**
5. **What can I do to lower my stress levels?**
6. **What can I do to make someone else's life better?**
7. **How can I change to improve my future?**

Doodles & Notes Page
Use and Enjoy

Reread the selection (if needed) and choose and circle the best answer to each question.

Connections Across Genres: Questions Part 2

1 All of the following similarities exists between the protagonists of *Frankenstein* (page 53) and *A Christmas Carol* (page 45) except –

   A   they both experience terror

   B   they both have a sense of disappointment in themselves

   C   they both have to learn a difficult lesson

   D   they both hide from their fears

E1.4(E)

2 The murder of Mercutio in *Romeo and Juliet* (page 93) could spark what modern debate?

   F   The right to bear arms

   G   The right to defend yourself

   H   The right of due process

   J   The freedom of expression

E1.4(E)

3 What purpose does the organizational pattern of *A Brief History of NASA* (page 129) and *The Pirates' Who's Who* (page 121) serve?

   A   To inform the reader on the lives of individuals within the passages

   B   To inform the reader on a series of sequential events

   C   To inform the reader on a series of unrelated events

   D   To inform the reader on the technologies developed within the passages

E1.4(H)

4 What literary element is present in both *The Pirates' Who's Who* (page 121) and *Romeo and Juliet* (page 93)?

    F Both use similes to represent the death of a character

    G Both use metaphors to represent the death of a character

    H Both have a character who is hot-headed and violent

    J Both have a character who is benevolent and tries to seek peace

E1.6

---

5 What do you predict will happen to the relationship between Diana and Enid in *He Said, She Said* (page 103), based on the reading passage?

    A The relationship between Diana and Enid will be strained

    B The relationship between Diana and Enid will be enhanced

    C The relationship between Diana and Enid will be ended

    D The relationship between Diana and Enid will remain the same

E1.4(E)

---

6 All of the following are differences between Poetry and Fiction texts except –

    F the use of text features that form the shape of the text on the page

    G the use of sensory details and vivid language

    H the description always includes imaginary events, people and / or places

    J the use of rhythm and / or rhyme within the text

E1.7

---

7 The authors attempt to _____ in the subject of both "If…" (page 71) and *A Christmas Carol* (page 45)?

    A   inspire motivation

    B   inspire change

    C   inspire improvement

    D   inspire fear

E1.8

Testing TIPS: The Science of Sleep and Breakfast

We know that parents and teachers always tell you to get a full night's sleep and to eat a good breakfast before a test. But, did you know that science actually backs this up?

Sleep on Success

Studies show that getting an adequate amount of sleep influences attention, memory and overall academic performance.

Benefits of Breakfast

1. Improved memory
2. Enhanced attention during school hours
3. Advanced verbal skills
4. Higher cognitive functioning
5. Increased performance on Multiple Choice Questions
6. Heightened inferencing and critical thinking skills

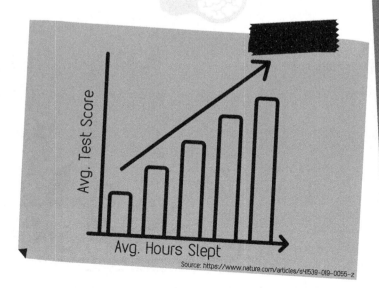

Doodles & Notes Page
Use and Enjoy

Written composition: Expository

Read the information in the boxes below.

"Some people teach you the worth of even a whispered Hello. Some, the value of a worded Goodbye."
 	
    -   Nitya Prakash
	"Some things cannot be taught; they must be experienced. You never learn the most valuable lessons in life until you go through your own journey."
	
	    - Roy T. Bennett

Which is more important, learning from someone or learning from your experiences? Think carefully about this question.

Write an essay about a success you had after making a change in your life.

Be sure to –

- Clearly state your <u>Thesis</u>
- <u>Organize</u> and <u>Develop</u> your <u>Ideas</u> effectively
- <u>Choose</u> your <u>Words</u> carefully

<u>Edit</u> your writing for <u>Grammar</u>, <u>Mechanics</u> and <u>Spelling</u>

Helpful Hint: Use this sheet for notes and to gather your thoughts before starting the essay – just like you should on the STAAR.

STAAR CHECKLIST

Expository Essay

	Yes	No	
Is there a clear thesis that restates and specifically addresses the prompt?	☐	☐ → **1**
↓
Does the writer attempt to develop ideas? (Avoids repetition)	☐	☐ → **1**
↓
Writing errors do not severely impact the fluency of the essay.	☐	☐ → **1**
↓
Ideas are well connected and address the writer's topic.	☐	☐ → **2**
↓
Writer supports thesis with _SPECIFIC_ persuasive evidence _THROUGHOUT_.	☐	☐ → **2**
↓
Can the essay be read smoothly?	☐	☐ → **2**
↓
Writer provides unique viewpoints/reflections.	☐	☐ → **3**
↓
Writer uses strong diction to promote purpose.	☐	☐ → **3**
↓
Sentence variety is used effectively.	☐	☐ → **3**
↓
		4

Review Questions Answer Key

This section is intended only for use during self-guided studying and / or when directed to by your teacher.

Remember, this study workbook will only be effective and help you **Ace the STAAR** if you use it seriously and answer each question on your own.

Don't cheat yourself!

1 What change, if any, needs to be made in Sentence 3?

   A Change the sentence to read: George Washington was the Commander in Chief of the Continental Army.

   B Change the sentence to read: By George Washington, who was the Commander in Chief of the Continental Army.

   C Change the sentence to read: The Commander in Chief of the Continental Army was George Washington.

   D Combine Sentences 2 and 3 to eliminate sentence fragment

Answer D is correct. Following the flow of the essay, this is the only answer that keeps the paragraph flow intact. **Answers A, B and C are all incorrect.** Although they may make the sentence fragment into a complete sentence (Subject – Verb – Object), none of these corrections work in the context of the overall paragraph.

E1.9(D)(i)

2 Which of the following sentences is an example of a run-on sentence?

   F Sentence 20

   G Sentence 11

   H Sentence 6

   J Sentence 4

Answer G is correct. Sentence 11 should be re-written to eliminate the run-on sentence by removing the unnecessary conjunction, **moreover,** and replacing it with proper punctuation and capitalization to create two sentences. **Answers F and H are distractors.** Although these sentences are long, they are not run-on sentences. **Answer J is incorrect.** This is simply a compound sentence.

E1.9(D)(i)

3 Which verb tense is used incorrectly?

   A **Kept** in Sentence 11

   B **Led** in Sentence 4

   C **Were** in Sentence 2

   D **Have** in Sentence 19

Answer A is correct. The past tense **kept** in Sentence 11 should be **keep** to match the present tense word **still**. These words currently have a verb tense disagreement. **Answers B, C** and **D are all incorrect.** Verb tense is used correctly in all of these sentences.

E1.9(D)(ii)

4 What change, if any, needs to be made in Sentence 7?

   F Add a comma after **disappointment**

   G Change **his** to **their**

   H Change **they** to **he**

   J No change should be made

Answer H is correct. The singular, masculine antecedent **his** does not agree with the pronoun **they** (plural). **They** should be changed to the singular, masculine pronoun, **he**. **Answer G is a distractor.** Although this change does fix the pronoun-antecedent disagreement, Sentence 6 clearly leads into Sentence 7 with the singular, masculine **Washington** and **he**. As Sentence 7 does not introduce anything to change the focus from singular to plural, this answer is not appropriate. **Answers F and J are incorrect.** Adding a comma after **disappointment** introduces an error into the sentence, and a change should be made due to the pronoun-antecedent error.

E1.9(D)(iii)

5 What change, if any, should be made to Sentence 5?

   A Change **fort** to **Fort**

   B Change **fourth** to **4th**

   C Change **fourth** to **Fourth**

   D No change should be made

Answer A is correct. Fort Necessity is a formal name and both words should be capitalized. **Answers B and C are distractors**. The sentence is not referring to the American holiday the Fourth of July, but is simply stating the date is the fourth day of July. **Answer D is incorrect**. The word **Fort** has a lower case 'F' that should be upper case.

E1.9(D)(iv)

---

6 What is the correct way to write Sentence 18?

   F If we seize this opportunity, learn from our mistakes, and develop new strategies we will eventually succeed.

   G If we seize this opportunity; learn from our mistakes, and develop new strategies, we will eventually succeed.

   H If we seize this opportunity, learn from our mistakes, and develop new strategies, we will eventually succeed.

   J If we seize this opportunity; learn from our mistakes, and develop new strategies we will eventually succeed.

Answer H is correct. This sentence correctly separates the items in the list and the dependent and independent clauses. **Answers F, G and J are incorrect**.   In answer F, the writer fails to separate the dependent clause from the independent clause. In answer G, the dependent and independent clauses are properly divided, however the semicolon is improperly used to separate items in a list within the dependent clause. In answer J, the semicolon is again used incorrectly, and the sentence fails to separate the dependent and independent clauses.

E1.9(D)(v)

---

7 What change, if any, should be made to Sentence 19?

   A Change the colon after **failures** to a comma

   B Change the colon after **failures** to a semicolon

   C Remove the colon after **failures**

   D No change should be made

Answer C is correct. The colon is improperly used in the sentence, and neither a comma nor a semicolon would be appropriate replacements. **Answers A and B are distractors**. Although changing the colon to a comma may seem correct at a glance, the resulting parenthetical phrase is incorrect as there is no need for a pause here. The semicolon replacement is incorrect as the phrase **is victory** is not an independent clause. **Answer D is incorrect**. The colon is an error in the sentence, so a change should be made.

E1.9(D)(v)

---

8 What change, if any, needs to be made in Sentence 20?

   F Add a comma after **that**

   G Change **begining** to **beginning**

   H Add a comma after **stronger**

   J No change is necessary

Answer G is correct. **Beginning** is misspelled in the sentence. **Answers F and H are distractors**. Placing a comma after the phrase **Understanding that**, leaves the reader with some amount of confusion as to what 'that' from the six preceding sentences is to be understood. Placing a comma after **stronger**, and before the **and** in a series results in an Oxford comma. This is not technically incorrect, but since this choice is optional and does not result in the correction of the misspelled word, it cannot be the most correct. **Answer J is incorrect**. Due to the misspelling of the word **beginning**.

E1.9(D)(vi)

9 Which of the following sentences contains a comma splice?

   A Sentence 11

   B Sentence 6

   C Sentence 10

   D Sentence 20

Answer C is correct. This sentence contains two independent clauses, joined by a comma, with no coordinating conjunction. **Answer A is a distractor**. This sentence is also a run-on sentence, but it is not a comma splice as it uses the conjunction, **moreover** between the two independent clauses. **Answers B and D are incorrect**. These sentences correctly use commas and conjunctions between independent and dependent clauses.

E1.9(D)(i)

Writing: Editing Lesson Questions Part 2 – My Best Self: Today, Tomorrow, Forever

---

1 What error was made in Sentence 10 and how can it be fixed?

   A Comma Splice – place a semicolon after the word **us**

   B Sentence Fragment – combine Sentences 9 and 10 with a comma

   C Verb Tense Consistency – change **struggle** to **struggled**

   D Pronoun – Antecedent Agreement – change **we** to **they**

Answer B is correct. Viktor has let this sentence fragment stand without connecting it to an independent clause. The best fix among the answers is to combine it with Sentence 9 as, "Tomorrow, and the next day, and the next; time is constantly moving forward, with or without us, so we must struggle against quitting or stopping." **Answers A, C and D are incorrect**. There is no comma splice because two dependent clauses are separated with a comma, not two independent ones. Both the Verb Tense and Pronoun Antecedent choices create even more confusion within this sentence fragment, they do not correct it.

E1.9(D)(i)

---

2 What is the correct way to write Sentence 13 in the active voice?

   F To become your best self is not easy

   G Your best self to become is not easy.

   H Becoming your best self is not easy.

   J No change – sentence already in active voice

Answer H is correct. This sentence is written in the active voice with the subject performing the answer. **Answers F, G and J are incorrect**. Each of these (including the original sentence) are forms of passive sentences, some (like Answer G), more awkward than others.

E1.9D(ii)

---

3 Which of the following words is misspelled?

   A The word **to** in Sentence 8

   B The word **fruition** in Sentence 11

   C The word **strength** in Sentence 14

   D The word **tomorrow** in Sentence 16

Answer A is correct. In this case, Viktor has used the words 'to late' to mean 'very late' or 'excessively late.' Thus, 'to' is misspelled as it should be spelled 'too.' **Answers B, C and D are incorrect**. These words are commonly misspelled, but they are all spelled correctly in the essay.

E1.9D(vi)

4 What is the best way to write Sentence 16?

  F I will live in the now today, tomorrow; forever.

  G I will live in the now today: tomorrow, forever.

  H I will live; in the now today, tomorrow, forever.

  J I will live in the now: today, tomorrow, forever.

Answer J is correct. This sentence correctly separates the thought, "I will live in the now" from its modifiers "today, tomorrow, forever." **Answers F, G and H are incorrect**. These answers all leave the phrase "now today" unseparated. This is at best awkward, and at worst forms a tautology (immediate repetition or duplication of meaning in a sentence).

E1.9D(v)

---

5 What change, if any, needs to be made in Sentence 2?

  A Insert a semicolon after Mahrer

  B Change **is guidance** to **was guidance**

  C Change **saint** to **Saint**

  D No change is needed in Sentence 2

Answer C is correct. Saint is part of the person's title, and thus must be capitalized. **Answers A, B and D are incorrect**. Inserting a semicolon after Mahrer treats this dependent clause like an independent clause. Changing the verb tense to was in front of guidance creates a mismatch between the words, "is a warning" and "was guidance." Finally, a change is needed due to the lack of capitalization on the word, Saint.

E1.9(D)(iv)

---

6 What error, if any, was made in Sentence 15 and how can it be fixed?

  F Fused Sentence – place a semicolon after the word **daily**

  G Pronoun – Antecedent Agreement – change **we are** to **I am**

  H Comma Splice – Divide 15 into two sentences at the word **now**

  J Sentence 15 does not contain an error

Answer G is correct. Viktor's use of the personal word **My** in the Antecedent requires a singular pronoun. The word **we** is plural and is best replaced with **I**. **Note:** the word **are** must also be replaced with the word **am** to correct this mistake. **Answers F, H and J are incorrect**. Placing a semicolon after the word **daily**, or anywhere in this sentence for that matter, is inappropriate because it is an independent clause with a list of dependent clauses. The same can be said of dividing the sentence into two at the word **now**. This results in an independent clause and a sentence fragment. Answer J is incorrect because of the Pronoun-Antecedent disagreement between **my** and **we**.

E1.9(D)(iii)

---

7 Where should quotations have been applied in the essay?

  A Around Sentence 12

  B Around Sentence 6

  C Around Sentence 17

  D Around Sentence 1

Answer D is correct. Sentence 2 identifies Sentence 1 as a saying attributed to Saint Mahrer. As such, it should be placed in quotations. **Answers A, B, and C are incorrect**. These are all personal statements or goals from Viktor, but these are not meant to be read as him speaking them aloud and thus requiring quotations.

E1.9(v)

194

8 What is the correct way to write Sentence 5?

   F What we do with each of those grains is entirely our choice.

   G What we do with each of those grains, was entirely our choice.

   H What we do with each of those grains, is entirely our choice.

   J What we do with each of those grains is, entirely our choice.

Answer F is correct. The words "What we do with each of those grains" is the subject of the sentence with the word **is** as its verb. No comma should be present between subject and verb, so this sentence is correctly written. **Answer J is a distractor.** Although it also maintains subject-verb before the comma, the comma placed after the verb is unnecessarily used. **Answers G and H are incorrect.** Both of these sentences separate subject from verb and therefore cannot be correct.

E1.9(D)(ii)

Writing: Revision Lesson Questions Part 1 – How Social Media has Affected Society

---

1 Sentence 2 is unclear. What change should Camila make to improve its clarity?

   A Change *worldwide* to **around the world**

   B Change *offer* to **offered**

   C Change *Those* to **These platforms**

   D Change *unlimited* to **endless**

Answer C is correct. As written, the word **those** can mean your phone or a social medial platform. Defining this word more closely helps key the reader in to the author's intended meaning. **Answers A, B and D are incorrect.** Answers A and D both provide synonyms for a word that neither changes its meaning nor its clarity. Answer B only changes the sentence to past tense, it does not add clarity to the sentence.

E1.9(C)

---

2 Camila wants to rewrite Sentence 7 to improve its support for topic Sentence 6. Which of the following sentences would best replace Sentence 7?

   F This can lead to engagement and dialogue with diverse people that was never possible in the pre-social media era.

   G I often find myself communicating with others through the use of these wonderful social media platforms.

   H Although social media can be used by everyone, it often reveals the darker side of our society and so could be harmful.

   J Sentence 7 already properly supports topic Sentence 6

Answer F is correct. Sentence 7, as written, is off topic and creates a misleading introduction to Sentence 8. Answer F provides both justification for the statement made in Sentence 6 as well as a proper, non-misleading transition into Sentence 8. **Answer H is a distractor.** This sentence may work in the introductory paragraph, but there is no context to support its use in line 7. **Answers G and J are incorrect.** Answer G remains off topic and still perpetuates the miscommunication in line 8. Answer J is incorrect because Sentence 7 as written is off topic.

E1.9(C)

3 Camila may have made a mistake in organizing her first paragraph. What change, if any, should be made to correct this?

A Move Sentence 3 in front of Sentence 5

B Delete Sentence 2

C Delete Sentence 4

D No change should be made

Answer C is correct. Sentence 4 is an unnecessary repetition of Sentence 3. As it adds no value to the paragraph, it should be removed. **Answers A, B and D are incorrect**. Answer A does not fix the repetition caused by Sentence 4; it only moves the order of the two repetitive sentences. Answer B removes important foundational information from the introductory paragraph and also does not fix the repetition. Answer D is incorrect because Sentence 4 should be removed to improve the overall paragraph.

E1.9(C)

---

4 Reread Sentences 7 – 8. Based on these sentences only, what does it appear Camila is inferring in Sentence 8?

F People around the world are more aware of issues and connected because of her

G People around the world are more aware of issues and connected because of social media

H People around the world are more aware of issues and connected than they were in the past

J People around the world are more aware of issues and connected because of their fellow man

Answer F is correct. Camila refers to her use of social media platforms in Sentence 7. Then she begins Sentence 8 with the phrase, **As a result**, indicating to the reader that the previous information, (in this case, Camila using social media platforms) has resulted in people becoming more connected and aware of issues. **Answer G and H are distractors**. Answer G is clearly the message Camila intended to convey, but her off-topic Sentence 7 spoils this interpretation for the reader. Answer H is a weak distractor that, based solely on Sentence 8 (vs 7 & 8), could be inferred. **Answer J is incorrect**. Answer J has no support within the essay, including Sentences 7 – 8.

E1.9(C)

---

5 Camila wants to change Sentence 12 to the active voice to help it flow better within the paragraph. How should Camila best change this sentence to make this revision?

A Social media helps improve society through awareness; whether through global communication with diverse people or by helping identify people in need.

B Whether through global communication with diverse people or by helping identify people in need, social media helps improve society through awareness.

C Improving society through awareness can be helped by social media; whether through global communication with diverse people or by helping identify people in need.

D Whether through global communication with diverse people or by helping identify people in need, awareness of society can be improved through social media.

Answer B is correct. This sentence correctly converts the passive sentence into an active sentence through the removal of **can be** and the reorganization to subject – action - object. **Answer A is a distractor**. This sentence is also written in the active voice, but contains a punctuation error between the independent and dependent clauses. **Answers C and D are incorrect**. Both of these answers remain in the passive voice.

E1.9(C)

196

6 Camila wants to add the sentence, **Social media is better and offers many advantages over older forms of communication.**, to her essay. Where is the best place to put this sentence?

    F Before Sentence 8

    G Before Sentence 13

    H Before Sentence 3

    J Before Sentence 6

Answer J is correct. This becomes the topic sentence for the second paragraph. The remaining sentences (minus 7 as the paragraph was originally written) provide support for this topic sentence. **Answer H is a distractor**. Although technically the sentence could work here, this location is not superior to placing the sentence before Sentence 6. **Answers F and G are wrong**. In neither location would this sentence add value.

E1.9(C)

---

7 What is the best example, if any, of parallel construction within the essay?

    A Use of **social media** in every paragraph

    B Use of **negative** in the first paragraph

    C Use of **better** in the conclusion

    D Parallel construction is not used in this essay

Answer C is correct. The word better is used in the conclusion repeatedly and in a parallel fashion to hammer home a thought of how social media has made people, neighbors and global citizens better. **Answer A is a distractor**. Although used multiple times within the three paragraphs, the words were never used in a parallel construction. **Answers B and D are incorrect**. The word negative is not used in a parallel manner and, due to the word better's parallel construction in the third paragraph, answer D is incorrect.

E1.9(C)

---

8 What is the most effective way to combine Sentences 10 and 11?

    F Nevertheless older forms of communication fall short, social media shines.

    G Where older forms of communication fall short, social media shines.

    H Despite older forms of communication falling short, social media shines.

    J Whenever older forms of communication fall short, social media shines.

Answer G is correct. In the previous paragraph, the downside of older communication (one-sided) was mentioned briefly, as well as how social media is better (two-way, global awareness, improved connection). By process of elimination, the word *Nevertheless* (indicating there was an argument for older forms of communication), *Despite* (indicating there was information about how social media filled a lack caused by older communication) and *Whenever* (indicating something was said about where older forms of communication did not fall short), are all less appropriate than the word *Where*. **Answer H is a distractor**. This answer could, with only a slight change to the second paragraph, be correct. As the second paragraph is currently written, it is incorrect. **Answers F and J are incorrect**. For the reasons noted about why Answer G is correct.

E1.9(C)

9 Camila has forgotten to include a thesis statement in her introductory paragraph. Which of the following sentences best characterize the message Camila was trying to communicate?

A Because of these potential detractors, social media hurts the growth of society with its ability to bridge the gaps of distance and open up harmful communication with diverse groups of people across the world.

B Even with these potential detractors, social media has improved society through its ability to bridge the gaps of distance and open up communication with diverse groups of people across the world.

C Because of these potential detractors, social media has made an impact on society through its ability to bridge the gaps of distance, and we may not be ready for open communication with diverse groups of people across the world.

D Even with these potential detractors, social media has made an impact on society through its ability to bridge the gaps of distance, but we may not be ready for open communication with diverse groups of people across the world.

Answer B is correct. This sentence properly transitions from the negatives described about social media in the preceding sentences to a fully supported thesis topic (how social media has improved society). **Answers C and D are distractors**. Both of these sentences transition the previous sentence and provide a thesis topic, but this topic is not fully supported by the following paragraphs. **Answer A is incorrect**. Although this sentence does provide a transition and a thesis statement, it is unsupported by the following paragraphs.

E1.9(C)

Writing: Revision Lesson Questions Part 2 - The Role Music Plays in our Culture and Lives

1 Joseph wants to add the dependent clause, **limited only by our imagination and experiences** to his essay. Where is the best place to add this clause?

A To the beginning of Sentence 2

B To the end of Sentence 26

C After **their voice,** in Sentence 10

D To the beginning of Sentence 16

Answer B is correct. The key to answering this type of question correctly is to add the dependent clause to each of the identified sentences to determine which method adds the most value. In this case, Sentence 26 becomes; **It offers an endless form of expression, limited only by our imagination and experiences**. Of the choices available, this adds the most value to the essay. **Answer D is a distractor**. Although the dependent clause will work with this sentence, it does not add as much value in amplifying the independent clause as in Sentence 26. **Answers A and C are incorrect**. In both instances there is a pronoun – antecedent issue between the words **our** and **their**.

E1.9(C)

---

2 Joseph would like to add the phrase, **Music, as a medium to express and exchange ideas, is stronger than written words.**, to strengthen his essay. Where should he add this phrase to best increase the coherence of his overall essay?

F Before Sentence 1

G Before Sentence 10

H Before Sentence 12

J Before Sentence 22

Answer H is correct. Placing this sentence before Sentence 12 sets up the comparison between how many read the newspaper and how many listen to music in Sentences 12 and 13. **Answer F is a distractor**. This sentence could indeed fit here to prepare the long comparison between how poetry was used like music is now used. However, Answer H is a superior choice and should be chosen. **Answers G and J are incorrect**. With Answer G, the sentence simply does not fit the flow of the paragraph and creates an awkward transition of thoughts if inserted before Sentence 10. With Answer J, using this as the topic sentence for the summary gives too much emphasis on the comparison between written words and music. This concept is not explored enough in the summarizing of the essay to warrant using this sentence at this location.

E1.9(C)

3 Which of the following is an example of parallel construction?

A Sentences 6 - 8

B Sentences 18 - 20

C Sentences 24 - 26

D All of the above

Answer D is correct. Sentences 6 – 8 use the word **before the** to initiate the parallelism. Sentences 18-20, use **When we're…we** to accomplish this effect. Sentences 24-26 use **It (verb)** to create the construction. **Answers A, B and C are incorrect**. The use of parallel construction in each of these sentences eliminate them from individually being the correct choice.

E1.9(C)

4 Joseph is worried his thesis sentence doesn't capture his main idea properly. What sentence below, if any, improves his thesis sentence succinctly and accurately to reflect his main ideas?

F Music is a forum for today's global generation and is better than poetry for letting people express how they feel.

G Music now gives voice to today's global generation and their struggles, providing for expression of everything from when they are born to when they struggle with life.

H Music now gives voice to today's global generation and their struggles, providing an endless forum for the expression of everything from birth to death.

J No change, the current thesis sentence already properly and succinctly reflects all main ideas

Answer H is correct. The paragraphs following the thesis statement provide examples about how music is everywhere around us throughout the globe and how it expresses everything we are going through. This answer best captures this concept while reducing the wordiness of the original thesis. **Answer F is a distractor**. This sentence was meant to key the student into its succinctness, but the essay touches on how poetry of old has become music of today and did not provide a comparison of which was better at expressing feelings. **Answers G and J are incorrect**. Both Answer G and the original thesis contain unnecessarily wordy dependent clauses starting with **providing**.

E1.9(C)

5 What change, if any, should Joseph make to improve the diction of Sentence 22?

A Remove the words **for me personally**

B Add a comma after **for me personally**

C Add a semicolon after **for me personally**

D No change should be made

Answer A is correct. Using both, **for me personally** and **I believe**, is redundant and should be avoided. **Answer B is a distractor**. Although technically this removes the punctuation error and is grammatically correct, this phrase remains redundant and unnecessary for the essay. **Answers C and D are incorrect**. Adding a semicolon after **personally** results in a punctuation error and, due to the redundant phrase, a change should be made.

E1.9(C)

6 After re-reading his introductory paragraph, Joseph believes Sentences 9 and 10 sound stilted and should be combined. What is the best way to combine these sentences?

    F Today we still find poems in our textbooks, and the voice of the young, their voice, still lyrical, is now musical.

    G Today we still find poems in our textbooks, as if the voice of the young, their voice, still lyrical, is now musical.

    H Today we still find poems in our textbooks, where the voice of the young, their voice, still lyrical, is now musical.

    J Today we still find poems in our textbooks, but the voice of the young, their voice, still lyrical, is now musical.

Answer J is correct. This answer comes from the conjunction used to connect the two independent clauses. Of the four, only 'and' and 'but' are coordinating conjunctions. Of these two, only the word *but* provides a proper transition to contrast what was to what is now. **Answer F is a distractor.** Although *and* is an appropriate coordinating conjunction, in this case, the author has provided a list to explain how things have changed since poetry was everything music is now. To best highlight that transition, using the word *but* is superior to *and*. **Answers G and H are incorrect.** Both of these sentences use subordinating conjunctions and subordinate the main point under the idea about poems. In the case of *as if*, this severely downplays the idea the author is trying to convey. In the case of *where*, it creates a potentially unclear statement; does the author mean that because we find poems in our textbooks, the voice of these poems is now lyrical and musical?

E1.9(C)

---

7 Joseph made a mistake organizing the second paragraph. What change should he make to correct this error?

    A Move Sentence 17 before Sentence 14

    B Move Sentence 16 before Sentence 14

    C Move Sentence 21 before Sentence 18

    D Move Sentence 20 before Sentence 18

Answer B is correct. Of the choices, this is the only one that adds value to the paragraph. This move allows Sentence 14 to provide examples of where music is intertwined as a universal language. **Answers A and D are distractors.** The move for Answer A could be used, but this would reduce the sentence's purpose of setting the introduction for the various 'things we're going through' and how they relate to different types of music. Answer D's sentence can also be moved, but this doesn't add value, it only changes the order of the three parallel items. **Answer C is incorrect.** This sentence cannot be moved before Sentence 18 as it uses the expression, **all these feelings**, referring to Sentences 18-20.

E1.9(C)

---

8 Joseph worries that Sentence 14 doesn't deliver his message effectively. What change, if any, would you make to Sentence 14 to improve its clarity?

    F Change the first *it's* to **music is**

    G Change both occurrences of the word *in* to **on**

    H Change the semicolons to commas

    J No change is needed

Answer F is correct. As the paragraph is currently written, it's could mean either **music is** or **the number is**. Changing **it's** to **music is** eliminates this clarity issue. **Answer G is a distractor.** Whether **in** or **on**, these words mean basically the same thing in the context of this sentence. **Answers H and J are incorrect.** Changing the semicolons to commas would introduce a multiple comma splice error. Also, the change is needed to improve the paragraph's clarity.

E1.9(C)

9 What sentence in the second paragraph does not add to its development?

    A Sentence 13

    B Sentence 15

    C Sentence 17

    D Sentence 20

Answer B is correct. Sentence 15, although an endorsement for the list of items in Sentence 14, adds very little value to the paragraph and is slightly off-topic. This sentence should be removed. **Answers A, C and D are incorrect**. Each of these sentences add to the development of the second paragraph's main idea that music is highly listened to and expresses the feelings of today's youth.

E1.9(C)

Fiction: Questions Part 1 – from *A Christmas Carol*

> "But for this, it would have been difficult to detach its figure from the night, and separate it from the darkness by which it was surrounded.
>
> He felt that it was tall and stately when it came beside him, and that its mysterious presence filled him with a solemn dread."

1 Based on this quotation from the reading passage, what can be inferred about the Ghost of Christmas Yet to Come?

    A The spirit is aggressive and menacing

    B The spirit is verbose and affable

    C The spirit is an ominous enigma

    D The spirit is genial and sympathetic

Answer C is correct. The narrator uses words like surrounded by darkness, mysterious and solemn dread. Thus ominous (impression of something bad about to happen, threatening) enigma (mysterious, difficult to understand) is the most correct response. **Answer A is a distractor**. Although the reader may connect the spirit with being menacing, with its dark, tall, mysterious presence; there is nothing in the quotation to indicate the spirit is aggressive. **Answers B and D are incorrect**. The spirit is not verbose (wordy) or affable (good natured), nor is it genial (cheerful) or sympathetic (pitying).

E1.6(B)

---

2 In Lines 8-10, the mood of the scene can best be described as –

    F gloomy

    G peaceful

    H nostalgic

    J festive

Answer J is correct. Multiple **festive** event references exist in the selection, including gleaming berries, mistletoe and the many types of food and drinks. **Answer H is a distractor**. Although Scrooge may indeed be **nostalgic** at seeing the festive change to his bedroom, nothing in the passage indicates this has occurred. **Answers F and G are incorrect**. The scene described is not **gloomy**, with its roaring fire and delicious steaming foods. Nor is the scene reliably **peaceful** with its glistening lights, mighty blaze and heaps of food.

E1.6(D)

---

3 By using the word, "shuffled" in Line 2, the author establishes Scrooge as being –

A apprehensive

B clumsy

C panic-stricken

D jubilous

Answer A is correct. Scrooge does not walk, stride, swagger or strut to the door, but he shuffles, dragging his feet. This would indicate he is **apprehensive** to see what is on the other side. **Answer C is a distractor.** There is nothing to indicate he is **panic stricken** as he takes full possession of his mind and gets up softly. **Answers B and D are incorrect.** He does not stumble or do anything similar to indicate he is **clumsy**, and he also does not show great joy as he heads towards the door to indicate he is **jubilous**.

E1.8(D)

> "It is always the person not in the predicament who knows what ought to have been done in it."

4 The irony of this quotation is that it calls attention to –

F people's tendency to assume they know what others should do

G hindsight always being 20-20

H Scrooge being in a predicament

J Scrooge's understanding of what should be done

Answer F is correct. This is a restatement of the quotation to clearly describe its irony. **Answer G is a distractor.** While in hindsight you may also know what ought to have been done, this quotation does not refer to hindsight. **Answers H and J are incorrect.** Scrooge is indeed in a predicament, but this is not stated ironically. The quotation also does not imply, let alone ironically imply, that Scrooge understands what should be done.

E1.8(E)

---

5 In Line 9, Dickens' description of a hearth known in Scrooge's time shows the author finds Scrooge to be –

A calculating

B impoverished

C unintelligent

D cold-hearted

Answer D is correct. By contrasting the mighty blaze currently in the hearth to the dull petrification of a hearth under Scrooge, the author is inferring the lack of warmth provided in Scrooge's time. The closest selection to this concept is **cold-hearted. Answer A is a distractor.** Although the reader may have formed their own opinion, there is nothing in Line 9 to indicate Scrooge is calculating. **Answers B and C are incorrect.** Scrooge's wealth and intelligence are not discussed anywhere in Line 9. Had the term been **miserly** rather than impoverished, then perhaps this answer would also be a distractor, but it would still not be correct, as the contrast in Sentence 9 is blaze to petrification, not generous to tightfisted.

E1.8(F)

6 In Line 27, the word, "Gravely" most likely means what?

F Ghostly

G Somberly

H Importantly

J Stately

Answer G is correct. The word **gravely** in this context is used to amplify the drama of the situation Scrooge faces as the Phantom approaches him. This is best expressed as: The Phantom slowly, **somberly**, silently approached. **Answers H and J are distractors**. Although **gravely** can mean seriously or somberly (gloomy or dull), neither **importantly** nor **stately** connect strongly enough to this meaning to warrant either of them being considered correct in the context of the sentence. **Answer F is incorrect**. The word **ghostly** may be a description of the Phantom, but it is not an appropriate meaning for the word **gravely**.

E1.2(B)

7 In Line 14, what is the closet definition to the word, "Dogged"?

A Determined, thorough

B Obstinate, pertinacious

C Rude, chivalrous

D Tenacious, hardworking

Answer B is correct. Both **obstinate** and **pertinacious** have the closest match to **dogged's** stubbornly determined meaning in the passage. **Answers A and D are distractors**. The word **determined** is an appropriate approximation to **dogged**, but the word **thorough** is not. Similarly, **tenacious** could be appropriate, but **hardworking** is slightly off subject. **Answer C is incorrect**. These two words have relatively opposite meanings, so are not a good pair as an answer.

E1.2

8 Based on the passage, what can be inferred about Scrooge's situation?

F Scrooge lives in a haunted house

G The spirits visit Scrooge to terrify him

H The spirits visit Scrooge to encourage change

J Scrooge has accidentally summoned two ghosts

Answer H is correct. Line 44 from the passage provides the best clue to this answer when Scrooge states he has fear, but he understands they have come to do him good and, "to (*make him*) be another man from what (*he*) was." **Answer G is a distractor**. Clearly Scrooge is frightened, but that is not the purpose of the spirits' visit. **Answers F and J are incorrect**. Nothing in the passage suggests Scrooge summoned the spirits, and, although his house does indeed appear to be haunted, this is not the main inference about his situation.

E1.4

9 In Line 26, by comparing the phantom to mist, the author is attempting to –

A use concrete details to describe the spirit

B show that the spirit is transparent

C describe the ghostly visage through sensory details

D personify mist to be phantom-like

Answer C is correct. The author has used sensory details to aid the reader in 'seeing' the Phantom glide towards Scrooge. **Answer A is a distractor**. The mist is indeed describing the spirit, more specifically the spirit's movement, but not in a concrete way. **Answers A and D are incorrect**. There is nothing to indicate the author means for the reader to think the spirit is transparent, indeed, the author uses details like draped and hooded to form a feeling that the Phantom is something of substance. The comparison of the phantom to mist is also not personifying the mist, but using it to describe a pattern of movement.

E1.8(D)

Fiction: Questions Part 2 – from *Frankenstein*

---

1 One can infer from this selection that the author's purpose for writing *Frankenstein* was to –

A entertain

B inform

C educate

D persuade

Answer A is correct. Based on the selection, it is clear that this work of fiction was made to entertain the reader. **Answers B and D are distractors**. Although these are potential purposes for writing, they are not correct for this selection. **Answer C is incorrect**. Educate is not one of the three purposes for writing. The purpose **inform** includes the purpose of educating.

E1.8(A)

---

2 The narrator's horror at his creation supports the author's message that –

F people can do anything that they put their mind to if they try

G science experiments can go horribly wrong

H new technology can be formed from old mistakes

J you must consider the consequences before acting

Answer J is correct. There are several statements throughout the passage that drive this response. The narrator calls his work a catastrophe, then states that accidents of life are not as changeable as emotions, then makes reference to two years of work turning into something the narrator disgusts. **Answer G is a distractor**. This science experiment has indeed gone wrong, but this is not the author's message. **Answers F and H are incorrect**. Although the narrator does mention how hard he worked to create the creature, the message is clearly not that people can do anything, but rather that people should beware what could result from their actions. Also, there is nothing in the passage to indicate the author desires the reader to believe that the narrator has created a new technology from his old mistakes.

E1.8(D)

---

3 Which line in the passage best describes its setting?

  A Line 9

  B Line 3

  C Line 18

  D Line 13

Answer B is correct. Line 3 sets the time (one in the morning) and place (location where it's raining, inside under low light) for the passage. **Answers C and D are distractors**. Although they both contain elements of setting, neither line is primarily focused on providing a setting for the passage. **Answer A is incorrect**. This line contains no element of setting.

E1.6(D)

> "I started from my sleep with horror; a cold dew covered my forehead, my teeth chattered, and every limb became convulsed; when, by the dim and
>
> yellow light of the moon, as it forced its way through the window shutters, I beheld the wretch—the miserable monster whom I had created."

4 This quotation contributes to which of the following moods?

  F Sorrowful and sanguine

  G Foreboding and regretful

  H Angry and dejected

  J Terse and choleric

Answer G is correct. The narrator wakes with a **foreboding** dread, exhibited by sweat on his forehead, his teeth chattering and his body convulsing. Then, he sees the monster and calls it a 'wretch,' identifying his **regret** at its creation. **Answers A and H distractors**. The narrator clearly feels **sorrowful** at creating the monster, but a **sanguine** (optimistic in hard situations) mood is not evident in this quotation. Also, the narrator may feel **dejected** (dispirited), but nothing indicates an **angry** mood. **Answer J is incorrect**. Neither a **terse** (abrupt) nor a **choleric** (bad-tempered) mood is evident in this quotation.

E1.8(F)

5 The author uses overstatement in Lines 24-26 to achieve what purpose?

  A To show the dramatic tendencies of the narrator

  B To compare the creature's malevolent nature to the narrator's nature

  C To describe the narrator's view of the monstrosity of the creature

  D To illuminate the narrator's intense fear

Answer C is correct. The author uses vivid, amplifying language to present the creature's monstrosity, with multiple overstatement's, such as 'no mortal', 'could not be so hideous' and 'Dante could not have conceived.' **Answer D is a distractor**. The narrator displays more a sense of awe than fear in these lines. **Answers A and B are incorrect**. There is perhaps a dramatic flair in the word choice used by the author, but this was not the author's purpose. Also, there is no comparison evident in these lines between the creature's nature and the nature of the narrator.

E1.8(G)

6 The author uses a simile in Line 9 to communicate what to the reader?

   F Accidents in life are similar to human feelings

   G Mistakes cannot be easily reversed

   H Errors can change human emotions

   J Flaws are the result of human passions

Answer G is correct. The author compares the ability of accidents and the ability of feelings to be changed, providing a stark contrast between the relative immutability of an accident and the fickleness of human feelings. **Answers F and H are distractors.** Clearly the author makes a connection between accidents in life and human feelings through the use of a simile, but this was not what the author was trying to communicate. Also, the author was not trying to communicate how errors can change human emotions, but that unlike human emotions, errors are hard to change. **Answer J is incorrect**. It is not evident that the author infers the mistake was a result of misplaced emotion in this line.

E1.6

---

7 This passage is a work of fiction characterized by all of the following except –

   A reader must infer the theme from the author's words

   B is based in reality with fabricated elements

   C has multiple, clear supporting details to develop a claim

   D uses strong imagery and symbolism

Answer C is correct. Using multiple, clear supporting details to develop a claim (a feature of argumentative text) does not characterize this work of fiction. **Answers A, B and D are incorrect**. These are all elements of a work of fiction and are evident throughout the passage.

E1.7

---

8 Which of the following inferences can be made on the significance of the narrator's dream in Lines 15-17?

   F The narrator misses Elizabeth

   G The creature reminds the narrator of his mother

   H Elizabeth will be horrified by the creature

   J Elizabeth's death is foreshadowed

Answer J is correct. The author vividly provides the contrast between life ('bloom of health') and clues to Elizabeth's impending death ('livid with the hue of death', 'a shroud enveloped her' and 'grave-worms crawling in'). **Answer F is a distractor**. Although the narrator may indeed miss Elizabeth, this is not the significance of the narrator's dream. **Answers G and H are incorrect**. There is no mention of the creature in these lines, so inferring the creature reminds the narrator of Elizabeth or that Elizabeth will be horrified by the creature is not appropriate.

E1.4(F)

1 What is the narrator's tone towards his intended audience?

   A Protective, fatherly

   B Pretentious, genuine

   C Warm, affable

   D Polite, enthusiastic

Answer A is correct. Throughout the poem, the narrator is providing advice on difficulties the reader may experience, how to deal with these situations and ends with 'my son', clearly showing a protective and fatherly tone to the intended reader. **Answers C and D are distractors**. There is no doubt that the narrator can be characterized as being warm and affable (friendly) in this poem. However, this friendliness takes on more of a fatherly tone given all the life advice and the chosen closing of the poem. Similarly, the narrator is very enthusiastic, especially in the closing, but the poem lacks polite-type phrases and displays a closer familial bond that polite words would lack. **Answer B is incorrect**. Although the narrator seems to be genuine, you cannot characterize the narrator as pretentious (trying to sound more important or smart than one is).

E1.8(F)

2 What is the purpose of the author's repetition of the word 'if' in the poem?

   F It suggest the narrator's advice is unnecessary

   G It highlights the narrator's fear for the audience's future

   H It emphasizes what the audience must do

   J It highlights the unlikeliness of the audience's success

Answer H is correct. The repeat of 'if' sets the conditions for the intended audience's success at the end (the world and everything in it, and becoming a man). **Answers G and J are distractors**. There is no evidence that the narrator is afraid for the intended reader. Likewise, the narrator does not make any judgement about the intended audience's likelihood of reaching the success identified at the conclusion of the poem. **Answer F is incorrect**. The narrator goes through great lengths to provide a life checklist for the intended reader to follow, not because the narrator exhibits vacuous thoughts, but because the narrator cares for the subject.

E1.7(B)

3 What does the poet personify in this quotation?

   A Thoughts

   B Truth

   C Two imposters

   D Triumph and Disaster

> If you can think—and not make thoughts your aim;
>
> If you can meet with Triumph and Disaster
>
> And treat those two impostors just the same;
>
> If you can bear to hear the truth you've spoken

Answer D is correct. Outcomes of life, triumph and disaster, are being personified as two imposters. **Answer C is a distractor**. The two imposters are being used to personify triumph and disaster. They are not being personified themselves. **Answers A and B are incorrect**. These words are not being personified and are being used concretely in this quotation.

E1.8(E)

4 What is the rhyme scheme of Stanza 4?

   F A, A, B, B, C, C, D, D

   G A, B, A, B, C, D, C, D

   H A, B, B, A, C, D, C, D

   J A, B, C, A, B, D, C, D

Answer G is correct. Note Lines 25 (virtue) and 27 (hurt you) form A; Lines 26 (touch) and 28 (much) form B; Lines 29 (minute) and 31 (in it) form C and Lines 30 (run) and 32 (son) form D to make the rhyme scheme. **Answer H is a distractor**. Although the C, D rhyme scheme is correct, the A, B scheme is misidentified. **Answers F and J are incorrect**. Neither of these two answers identify any area of the rhyme scheme correctly.

E1.8

---

5 What aspect of life is referenced in Lines 13-16?

   A Challenges, distractions

   B Love, camaraderie

   C Old age, death

   D Defeat, loss

Answer D is correct. The narrator's two conditions in these lines are bearing up against words being twisted into something the intended audience did not expect, and rebuilding after losing (through brokenness) things the intended reader had given their life to creating. **Answer A is a distractor**. Clearly while the intended reader is dealing with these issues, they would be considered challenging and distracting. However, the narrator does not classify these as mere distractions (diversion, something that prevents full attention, agitation), but rather something that would cause the intended reader to build up again a life's worth of work. **Answers B and C are incorrect**. Neither love nor camaraderie are inferenced in the lines. Also, there is no mention of age or death (life is used to indicate the intended reader would have put a portion of their life to accomplishing a task, not that the intended would experience death).

E1.4(E)

---

6 What is the symbolic meaning of "heart and nerve and sinew" on Line 21 of the poem?

   F Hope and determination and strength

   G Romance and intelligence and ferocity

   H Courage and attitude and health

   J Love and confidence and muscle

Answer F is correct. The second half of Stanza 3, starting at Line 21 revolves around the power the 'Will' has to keep going even when our motivations and strength are lost. Kipling uses the phrase "heart and nerve and sinew" not as literal parts of the body, but metaphorically to mean 'your hopes, desires, confidence, determination and strength to continue.' **Answer J is a distractor**. This answer provides a close approximation to the reasoning provided for Answer F, except for the word muscle, which is closer related to the concrete meaning of the word strength than its abstract meaning. **Answers G and H are incorrect**. These answers are both slightly off-topic and do not provide an adequate symbolic meaning for the author's words.

E1.4(D)

1 Which lines in the poem best highlight the narrator's obsession with Annabel Lee?

A Lines 38 - 39

B Lines 5 - 6

C Lines 15 - 16

D Lines 27 - 28

Answer A is correct. In these lines, the narrator characterizes Annabel as 'his life' and states that every night he lies down beside her tomb. **Answer D is a distractor.** In these lines the narrator is describing how strong their love was, rather than demonstrating the obsession shown in Lines 38-39. **Answers B and C are incorrect.** In Lines 5-6, the narrator explains how Annabel Lee felt about him. Lines 15-16 have even less relevance as they simply state that Annabel Lee was chilled by a cold wind.

E1.8(D)

2 The narrator's reference to Annabel's kinsmen as "highborn" implies that –

F he is highborn as well and is deserving of respect

G Annabel Lee rules the kingdom they live in

H they did not approve of his relationship with Annabel Lee

J he is lowborn and should be pitied

Answer J is correct. In even using the word 'highborn' to describe Annabel's kinsmen, the narrator implies they are something the narrator is not. Another 'highborn' person would not need to state this as it would be assumed. His addition of the words, "bore her away **from me**" is the narrator's call for the reader to pity his loss of Annabel to the kinsmen. **Answer H is a distractor.** The narrator provides that the kinsmen took Annabel away due to her being chilled by a cold wind. It could possibly be interpreted at this point in the poem that the cold wind could be a change to chilled feelings towards the narrator and the kinsmen 'rescued' Annabel, but this implication soon fades as the stanza ends with Annabel locked in a tomb ("sepulchre") by the sea. **Answers F and G are incorrect.** As stated earlier, a highborn would not need to announce this, but if the narrator was highborn and 'deserved respect', he would announce it with some form of pompous wording that is lacking in the stanza. Similarly, nothing indicates Annabel rules the kingdom, only that the narrator and Annabel live in a kingdom (although this kingdom is likely entirely of the narrator's making.)

E1.8(F)

3 The narrator mentions "wingèd seraphs." What is a synonym for seraph?

A Deity

B Angel

C Demon

D Spirit

Answer B is correct. A Seraph is an important angel; thus, angel is the most appropriate synonym. **Answer A is a distractor.** Although some definitions of seraph may state they are celestial beings, they are not considered deities. **Answers C and D are incorrect.** Seraph are not defined by either of these terms.

E1.2(A)

4 Based on the poem, what can we infer the narrator believes killed Annabel Lee?

   F The kinsmen

   G The plague

   H The wind

   J The angels

Answer J is correct. The clue to this answer lies in Lines 21-26. Summarized: Angels, not happy and envying them, were the reason the wind came to chill and kill Annabel Lee. **Answer H is a distractor**. The wind was clearly used as the murder weapon, but the narrator places the blame on the angels "as all men know" for the deed. **Answers F and G are incorrect**. Taking the poem in its entirety, the kinsmen took Annabel Lee after she had already died and placed her in a tomb, so they cannot be the cause of death. As for the plague, it is more likely that hypothermia killed Annabel Lee as there are no words like pox or black death, that would commonly be used to indicate plague at the time, and many references to her being chilled.

E1.2(B)

---

5 Which of the following statements would the narrator most likely agree with?

   A Love is more painful than death

   B Love ends with death

   C Love never dies

   D Love and death are interchangeable

Answer C is correct. In Lines 30-33, the narrator states nothing, heaven or demons, can tear their souls apart. He backs these words with his actions in 38-41 when he sleeps by her tomb every night. **Answer B is a distractor**. The death of Annabel Lee is clear within the poem. However, the love the narrator continues to exhibit for her, even after her death, is also clearly evident. **Answers A and D are incorrect**. Throughout the narrator's obsessive behavior, he never once complains that love is painful, and despite his sleeping with his dead bride at her tomb, there is no evidence the narrator believes love and death are interchangeable.

E1.8(A)

---

6 What can the reader infer as to the true cause of Annabel's death?

   F Hypothermia

   G Supernatural forces

   H Jealous angels

   J Cold wind

Answer F is correct. Annabel's death was caused, as the narrator states twice, by her being chilled by the cold wind. This likely caused her to go into Hypothermia (low body temperature) which, untreated, is often fatal. **Answer J is a distractor**. The cold wind was a contributing factor in Annabel's death, rather than the true cause. **Answers G and H are incorrect**. The narrator does blame the death on supernatural forces, specifically jealous angels, but the true cause of death was almost certainly more natural and the result of Annabel being chilled to a dangerously low body temperature.

E1.4(F)

1 What is meant by "house" in Mercutio's words "A plague o' both your houses!"?

  A Dwelling

  B Extended family

  C Government building

  D Political party

Answer B is correct. Mercutio is, rightfully so, placing blame for his injury on the feud between the families of the Montagues and the Capulets. In his statement, "A plague o' both your houses!", he is cursing the extended families of both 'Houses.' **Answer D is a distractor**. Although the Montagues and the Capulets would certainly have their own political agendas, they are recognized by their familial name and not by their political parties. **Answers A and C are incorrect**. The word 'house' in Mercutio's speech is not a simple dwelling or a government building, but rather represents two entire families based on their last name.

E1.7(A)

2 Tybalt's grudge against Romeo resulted in Mercutio's demise. What is the author's intended message concerning these events?

  F Danger can come even when least expected

  G The impact of hatred spreads beyond the concerned parties

  H Conflict is often unjustified and one-sided

  J It is better to mediate a conflict than to escalate it

Answer G is correct. The feud between the two houses fueled the grudge between Tybalt and Romeo that, in Act 3, Scene 1, led to Mercutio's death. Mercutio, although a friend of Romeo, was "the prince's near ally" (actually related to the royal house) and not a Montague like Romeo. Thus, the hatred of the two warring houses spread beyond the bounds of its familial ties to impact outsiders and friends. **Answers F and H are distractors**. Although, in Mercutio's case, danger did come unexpectedly from beneath Romeo's arm, this underhanded attack was not the author's intended message. There is also minimal justification for the violence given in Act 3, Scene 1, but the conflict is certainly characterized as two-sided, ultimately between Tybalt and Mercutio. **Answer J is incorrect**. This may be a true statement, but the negative outcome from Romeo's attempt to mediate the conflict between Tybalt and Mercutio shows this is not the author's message.

E1.6(A)

3 Mercutio and Tybalt are Character Foils. How are these two individuals best characterized?

  A Tybalt and Mercutio are hot-headed

  B Tybalt and Mercutio are light-hearted

  C Tybalt is light-hearted; Mercutio is hot-headed

  D Tybalt is hot-headed; Mercutio is light-hearted

Answer D is correct. Tybalt initiates a conflict with Romeo, calling him villain and responding to Romeo's attempt to deescalate the situation with a call for Romeo to draw his weapon. Mercutio, on the other hand, uses comedic, lighthearted phrases and metaphors, such as calling Tybalt a "rat-catcher" and "king of cats" and brushing off even his mortal wound as only "a scratch." **Answer C is a distractor**. Although this answer identifies the two opposites essential in a character foil, the actual characterizations are wrongly assigned. **Answers A and B are incorrect**. As the characterizations for both Tybalt and Mercutio are the same, these are examples of mirror characters, not character foils.

E1.6(B)

4   What dramatic convention below most closely identifies the technique Shakespeare uses in Lines 61 – 69?

   F   Monologue

   G   Aside

   H   Dramatic Irony

   J   Soliloquy

Answer A is correct. Although slightly on the short side for a monologue, this is the only term that applies. **Answer H is a distractor**. While irony is clearly displayed in Lines 62-63, this a verbal irony, not dramatic irony. **Answers G and J are incorrect**. The speaker is not speaking to the audience as an aside, but to the characters around him. Also, Mercutio is not speaking his own thoughts aloud, but rather speaking about his injury and railing Romeo for his interference.

E1.7(C)

---

5   What is the significance of the color 'black', modifying fate on Line 89?

   A   Evokes sensory details of the settings

   B   It is an omen of terrible events to come

   C   It is a message of fate being evil

   D   It describes Romeo's emotional state

Answer B is correct. Romeo is expressing how the death of Mercutio will spark additional terrible events. In this line, he foreshadows the tragedies yet to come, ending with his and Juliet's death. **Answer D is a distractor**. Romeo may indeed be in a 'black' mood at this point, only just realizing he has lost a friend, and it was, in large part, his fault. However, if intending to attribute this blackness to Romeo and not to future events, Shakespeare would likely have used something akin to Romeo's black countenance, or similar metaphor, to drive the reader to believe Romeo is depressed. **Answers A and C are incorrect**. There is a limited reference to setting (time perhaps), but not any darkness as a setting that the color black might modify. Also, there is not any personification of fate being evil. Romeo is simply stating that a dark (bad, foreboding, terrible) fate is coming due to the events of the day.

E1.8(D)

> Will you pluck your sword out of his scabbard by the ears?

6   Shakespeare uses what literary device in this quotation?

   F   Simile

   G   Personification

   H   Allusion

   J   Hyperbole

Answer G is correct. Shakespeare, by giving a sword ears to be plucked out by, is personifying the sword. **Answer A is a distractor**. Although a comparison (likely between the hilt of the sword and a man's ears) is being made, this is done through a metaphor, not a simile. **Answers H and J are incorrect**. Shakespeare is not hinting at anything beyond the sword at this point, so there is no allusion evident. Similarly, there is no evidence of a hyperbole (exaggeration beyond literal meaning), such as, 'the street was wide as the ocean,' or other such exaggerations.

E1.8(E)

7 What does Mercutio mean by "a grave man" in Line 63?

    A A sad man

    B A stoic man

    C An angry man

    D A dead man

Answer D is correct. Mercutio is literally joking that the wound is bad enough to kill him. Loosely translated, he's saying, 'The wound isn't too deep or wide, but it's enough to kill me. By tomorrow, I will be dead in the grave.' **Answers A and C are distractors**. While grave on its own may be translated as sad or somber (a grave man = a sad or somber man), in this context Mercutio clearly means dead. Similarly, although he is clearly angry at the moment, with multiple curses of plagues on Romeo and Tybalt's houses, there is no evidence Shakespeare intended to have 'grave' translated to angry. **Answer B is incorrect**. With the amount of complaining about his wound he has already done (albeit with cause), it is unlikely, were Mercutio to survive, he would present himself stoically (enduring pain without feeling or complaint) the next day.

E1.2(B)

---

8 Using contextual clues, what is a synonym for "bandying" in Line 45.

    F Loitering

    G Arguing

    H Fighting

    J Gambling

Answer H is correct. Given that Line 45 occurs in the middle of a fight Romeo is trying to stop, this contextually lends to this conclusion. In addition, as the term 'bandying' means to give and take, trade or exchange, and the characters could be described as bandying blows with their swords, the definition meaning lends to this inference. **Answer G is a distractor**. While the characters, especially Tybalt and Mercutio, are clearing arguing, both before and during the swordfight, Romeo is not trying to break up an argument in Line 45, but a clash of swords. **Answers F and J are incorrect**. The characters are not loitering (standing around) in the streets, nor are they gambling in this scene.

E1.2(C)

Drama: Questions Part 2 – from *He Said, She Said*

---

1 Using the dialogue between the three women, the author makes a critique on what human tendency?

    A Marriage

    B Gossip

    C Jealousy

    D Socializing

Answer B is correct. From Line 1, gossip about what someone said about someone else is in the forefront of this passage. The conflict resulting from the either malicious or miscommunicated gossip is the focus of the entire selection. **Answer C is a distractor**. There is an element of jealousy among the three women, but the rumors used by the three women and the results of those rumors are the focus of the author's critique. **Answers A and D are incorrect**. While near the end of the passage, it becomes clear that at least one of the rumors is centered around who Felix wanted to marry, marriage in and of itself is not being critiqued in those lines. Also, the author is clearly using socializing between the characters to provide the backdrop for the story, but socializing itself is not being examined.

2 The final line of the passage characterizes Felix as –

   F dense

   G earnest

   H oblivious

   J inconsiderate

Answer H is correct. Although he has stood by during the entire conversation between the three women, he has obviously been completely oblivious to the finer points. This becomes clear when he answers with, "I don't know what you're talking about." **Answers F and J are distractors.** While his answer on this line may seem dense, the author has not characterized Felix as so, and in the stage directions immediately prior to this answer, states he answers foolishly, leading one to believe he was caught in the moment unaware versus being too dense to answer correctly. While an argument can be made that ignoring the words of someone (let alone three people) talking in a group you are a part of is inconsiderate, the other side of that argument is that he was politely minding his own business. It wasn't until the end, when the women turned to him for answers that he stumbled on his words from his sideline view. **Answer G is incorrect.** Felix, oblivious to the argument surrounding him (which he was directly connected to by words attributed to and about him), was certainly not earnest (sincere, intense).

E1.6(B)

---

3 How does the setting impact the overall story?

   A It shows the reader Felix's background story

   B It allowed for Diana and Enid to share information

   C It produces a mood of light-hearted banter

   D It enabled the social interaction that resulted in a conflict

Answer D is correct. The setting of a party or social gathering at Enid's home is the backdrop for the rumormongering happening by the three women at different occasions prior to the quarrel evident in the scene. **Answer B is a distractor.** Diana and Enid did share information within the quarrel, and though they may have shared information prior to the conflict, there is no evidence of this occurring. Enid and Mrs. Packard were together sharing information (gossip) when the conflict between the three women began. **Answers A and C are incorrect.** Almost no information about Felix (with the exception of some gossip about who he was romantically inclined towards), is provided in the passage. Also, the exchange is anything but light-hearted, with it's heated, emotional words and almost constant interruptions.

E1.6(D)

---

4 What do the dashes on the ends of lines throughout the passage indicate?

   F Interruptions

   G Trailing off of the speaker's words

   H Intentional syntax by the author

   J Emotional pauses

Answer F is correct. The dashes indicate where the next speaker cuts the current speaker off. Imagine an argument you've had and think back to when you were speaking and someone cut in with their own words without letting you finish. This is the emotional type of exchange the author is developing through the use of this syntax. **Answers H and J are distractors.** Clearly this use of syntax was intentional by the author. However, these dashes were not done simply for aesthetics and the desires of the author. Also, if the author had provided context to each character's thoughts within the passage, the dashes could be used as reflective or emotional pauses. As written, however, the immediate and passionate dialogue from other speakers occurring right after them indicates an interruption rather than an introspection. **Answer G is incorrect.** It is clear that the speakers had more to say if they had the time to get the words out. As each speaker struggles to get their words in over the other, the other speakers are interrupted, not trailing off.

E1.7(C)

214

5 The lines inside of [brackets] are called –

A scenes

B acts

C stage directions

D dialogue

Answer C is correct. Within a drama, words written within [brackets] standing alone are stage directions. These words are used to provide the actors with information on how to act, where to go and how to speak. **Answer D is a distractor**. Although this drama is full of dialogue between characters, the bracketed stage directions only have information for the actors, not dialogue. **Answers A and B are incorrect**. A scene is a subdivision of the major division act. These are indicated at the top of the Act and Scene. For example, from the *Romeo and Juliet* passage, Act III: Scene 1.

E1.7

---

6 The parallel construction used in Lines 6 – 8 indicates that Diana may be feeling –

F disdain

G paranoid

H infatuation

J relieved

Answer G is correct. Diana's repeated use of the word, 'perhaps', is her way of going through multiple negative scenarios without knowing if they have any basis in the truth, a form of paranoia. **Answer F is a distractor**. While clearly considering many possibilities of what has been said and thought, there is no indication Diana has disdain (finding unworthy of consideration or respect) for Enid in these lines. **Answers H and J are incorrect**. Infatuation (intense admiration) for Enid (or anyone else for that matter) is not displayed within Lines 6 – 8. Being relieved (no longer feeling distressed) is also quite the opposite of how Diana appears to feel in these lines.

E1.6

Informational: Questions Part 1 – from *The Pirates' Who's Who*

---

1 Clues to the organizational pattern used in this passage and its structure include –

A the words: *Roberts began* (Line 2), *He then* (Line 6) and *The end* (Line 16) creating a Sequence and Order text structure

B the words: *Roberts's speech* (Line 1), *to revenge* (Line 2) and *April, 1721* (Line 12) creating a Description text structure

C the words: *justifiable death* (Line 2), *devastating the* (Line 8) and *was hit* (Line 22) creating a Cause and Effect text structure

D the words: *since he* (Line 1), *went north* (Line 9) and *thrown overboard* (Line 23) creating a Problem and Solution text structure

Answer A is correct. Like many informational texts, this passage is written in a Sequence and Order manner, spanning the time period where Roberts first started pirating until his death. **Answer B is a distractor**. There is certainly a descriptive nature in this passage, but as it covers a time period with descriptions of what happened during that time period, rather than simply being the who, what, why, etc. of the subject, it best follows the Sequence and Order text structure as previously described. **Answers C and D are incorrect**. If you try hard enough, you can find some cause and effect within the passage – for example, the death of Roberts' captain led to him becoming a pirate, then terrorizing the sea, and ultimately dying. You can also, with a stretch, find some problem and solution – for example, since he was a pirate, he needed ships to attack safely, so he went north to terrorize Newfoundland. This, of course, is more something that can be inferred than the overall structure.

E1.8(B)

2 What did the author mean when he wrote, "played the very devil" in Line 9?

    F   Roberts was devil-like in his appearance

    G   The English and French fishing fleets and settlements were superstitious of the pirates

    H   He devastated the English and French fishing fleets and settlements

    J   Roberts used his reputation to convince the English and French fishing fleets and settlements he was a devil

Answer H is correct. The author is using a metaphor and an informal writing style to convey that Roberts, upon reaching Newfoundland, terrorized the English and French fleets and settlements there. **Answer J is a distractor**. While almost assuredly Roberts' reputation preceded him, there is nothing in the passage to concretely determine the English and French were convinced he was a devil. **Answers F and G are incorrect**. The passage does not speak a single word about Roberts' appearance. It also does not mention anything about the superstitions of the French and English.

E1.8(D)

---

3 All of the following characteristics of the Informational Text genre are included in the passage except -

    A   it includes facts, and is not based in the author's opinions

    B   it is based on reality with fabricated characters, situations or settings

    C   it is structured and concise with an easy-to-read layout

    D   it uses clear, unambiguous language to easily convey the information

Answer B is correct. This is a characteristic of a work of fiction. **Answers A, C and D are incorrect**. All of these are characteristics of Informational Texts and are evident in the passage.

E1.7(D)

---

4 One can infer from this selection that the author's purpose for writing *The Pirates' Who's Who* was to –

    F   inform

    G   persuade

    H   entertain

    J   confirm

Answer F is correct. Although written in a welcoming, informal manner, the overall purpose of this text is to inform the reader about the lives of pirates. **Answer H is a distractor**. Unlike some Informational Texts, this passage was written in a witty, enjoyable way, but its main purpose was not to entertain, but to inform. **Answers G and J are incorrect**. The author does not try to persuade the reader for or against Roberts, but almost neutrally presents the facts of his pirating life. Answer J is not one of the three purposes for writing.

E1.8

---

5 What point of view does the author use in this passage from *The Pirates' Who's Who*?

    A   1st Person

    B   2nd Person

    C   3rd Person-omniscient

    D   3rd Person-limited

Answer D is correct. This work of nonfiction was written based on things that had been revealed to the narrator and written using he and his statements indicative of the 3rd person. **Answer C is a distractor**. The narrator was not at the events, nor did he have knowledge of everything surrounding the events, but relied on information provided by eyewitnesses to others. **Answers A and B are incorrect**. The narrator did not explain the happenings from his own viewpoint, nor did he speak directly to the audience, but stuck to the he and his statements of the 3rd person point of view.

E1.8

6 The author did not create a formal thesis for this passage. Which of the following sentences would best describe the main idea of the passage to provide a thesis?

F Roberts was a pirate in the 1700's who plundered towns, ships and settlements until he died.

G Roberts, a notorious pirate in the 1700's, was killed during a battle at Parrot Island.

H Roberts plundered and fought throughout his pirating career in the 1700's, ultimately dying as he lived, fighting.

J Roberts, a pirate in the 1700's, was caught with his crew unprepared to fight and died during a battle at Parrot Island.

Answer H is correct. Reference back to Sentence 24 – Answer H's version of the thesis statement best ties to this restatement in the summary and characterizes Roberts overall career. **Answer F is a distractor**. Answer F is a suitable thesis, but Answer H includes a closer tie to the concluding paragraph and is superior. **Answers G and J are incorrect**. Both answers G and J drive the thesis main idea to Roberts' death at Parrot Island. Although this is discussed near the end of the passage, the fighting and pillaging of his career are the primary focus.

E1.7(D)(i)

---

7 Which of the following sentences does not support the author's main idea in this passage?

A Sentence 22

B Sentence 12

C Sentence 2

D Sentence 1

Answer D is correct. Sentence 1, when put under the context of the passage, seems to add little value. One supposes this is the author's hook, but the speech itself is not put into context of when it occurred, somewhat spoiling the author's sequence of events structure. **Answers A, B and C are incorrect**. These sentences are key to the main idea of the passage; framing Roberts' career, starting with his first attack, then moving to his return to Guinea and finishing with his death.

E1.7(D)(i)

---

8 Which of the following sentences, based on the overall theme of the message, provides the best conclusion?

F Sentence 23

G Sentence 24

H Sentence 25

J Sentence 26

Answer G is correct. Sentence 24 provides closure to the overall passage, and is the best conclusion of the options. **Answers F, H and J are incorrect**. Sentence 23 provides continuing details that were not previously provided, so cannot be a summarizing sentence. Sentences 25 and 26 form the author's 'thought-provoking' concluding statement.

E1.7(D)(i)

1 What evidence within the graphic demonstrates a Sequence and Order structure?

   A   Evolution of technology

   B   Women and tweets in space

   C   Use of dates

   D   The graphic is not in a Sequence and Order structure

Answer C is correct. The use of an increasing timeline of dates clearly marks this graphic as a Sequence and Order structured document. **Answers A, B and D are incorrect**. The evolution of technology, although it might be inferred from the student's knowledge of technology, is not discussed on the graphic. Also, neither women nor tweets help establish a Sequence and Order structure on their own, rather, this is established with a corresponding timeline. Finally, Answer D is incorrect because of the use of the timeline within the graphic.

E1.7(D)

2 What can we infer about the author's message from the graphic?

   F   Space has changed a lot since NASA started

   G   NASA accomplished much and had some challenges in its first half century

   H   In 52 years, NASA went from being created to sending tweets in space

   J   Sally Ride was the first woman in space

Answer G is correct. The author's message clearly is to highlight some highs and lows to demonstrate the accomplishments and challenges from NASA's first 50 years. **Answer H is a distractor**. This answer is simply restating the facts provided, i.e., no inference is required to make this statement as this information is stated plainly in the text. **Answer F and J are incorrect**. It could be inferred that *NASA* has changed a lot since it started, but there is no mention on the graphic about how *space* has changed. Also, the graphic does not provide enough information to infer that Sally Ride was the first woman in space. It only provides the fact that she was the first *American* woman in space.

E1.8(A)

3 How does the organizational pattern of this graphic support the its message?

   A   Provides a series of events to give a glimpse of NASA's failures

   B   Provides a series of events to give a glimpse at NASA's accomplishments

   C   Provides a series of events to give a glimpse at NASA's historic moments

   D   Provides a series of events to give a glimpse of NASA's important people

Answer C is correct. The graphic provided NASA's historical moments, including accomplishments, failures and important people. **Answer B is a distractor**. While clearly the bulk of the graphic focused on NASA's accomplishments, the Challenger incident would not be counted among them. **Answers A and D are incorrect**. These are both only part of what this organizational pattern provided to the reader.

E1.7(D)(ii)

4 How do the print features of the graphic enhance its effectiveness?

    F   Provide concrete examples of NASA's past events

    G   Provide abstract examples of NASA's past events

    H   Provide concrete examples of NASA's ambitions

    J   Provide abstract examples of NASA's ambitions

Answer F is correct. Each of the print features accurately provides a date and a description of the occurrence for that date in NASA's history. **Answer G is a distractor**. The events are told concretely, not abstractly – for example, *Sally Ride became the first American woman in space* versus *Sally Ride rode to the stars*. **Answers H and J are incorrect**. There was no discussion of NASA's ambitions anywhere within the graphic.

E1.8(C)

---

5 How do the graphic features of this graphic enhance its effectiveness?

    A   Provide an accurate rendering of described events to increase reader visualization

    B   Provide a correlated rendering of described events to increase reader visualization

    C   Demonstrate effective use of tone to enhance the author's message

    D   Demonstrate effective use of mood to enhance the author's message

Answer B is correct. While the images were not accurate representations of the described events, they were still effective at increasing the reader's visualization of the events. **Answer A is a distractor**. Had photos of the events and items related to the described events been used, this answer would be correct, however, none of the pictures are truly accurate to their coordinated text. **Answers C and D are incorrect**. Mood and tone were not developed by the graphics.

E1.8(C)

---

6 Which of the events listed on the graphic most likely had the greatest impact on NASA?

    F   January 22, 2010

    G   January 28, 1986

    H   July 20, 1969

    J   October 1, 1958

Answer J is correct. None of the other events, no matter how significant, would have happened without NASA first being established. **Answers G and H are distractors**. While no doubt each of these events were very historical, NASA's establishment was ultimately responsible for both events. **Answer F is incorrect**. A tweet, or any other digital transmission from space, pales in importance to any of the other events listed.

E1.4

1 Which sentence below correctly describes the organizational pattern used by Kennedy in this speech?

A   Kennedy provided a chronological sequence to identify the ordering of his message

B   Kennedy examined the similarities and differences of nations to frame his message

C   Kennedy defined a problem and provided solutions to form his message

D   Kennedy described major components of a topic to deliver his message

Answer C is correct. Kennedy defined a problem (to assure survival and success of liberty) and provided numerous examples of how America will overcome and meet that goal (loyalty to friends, help for struggling countries, support for the United Nations, peace with adversaries while remaining strong militarily, etc.) **Answer B is a distractor.** While Kennedy did indeed examine several types of nations (old allies, new free states, struggling nations, border nations, etc.), this was not done in a compare and contrast way, only as a way to introduce them in his speech. **Answers A and D are incorrect.** There was no form of chronological sequence evident in the speech and, although he did describe some features within his speech, it was clearly not dedicated to describing the who, what, when, where and how of his topic, but rather was dedicated to describing how to meet the goals outlined in his opening statement.

1.8(B)

---

2 What did Kennedy mean by *forum for invective* in Sentence 15?

F   Place where people meet to discuss inventions

G   Place where people meet to argue and criticize

H   Place where people join together for business meetings

J   Place where people join together for casual meetings

Answer G is correct. Kennedy was outlining how America's support for the United Nations would help prevent it from becoming an assembly of only conflict and criticism between nations. Thus, invective was used concretely here, meaning 'highly critical language or insults.' **Answers F, H and J are incorrect.** While 'meet' and 'join together' may be considered synonyms for *forum*, neither 'inventions', 'business meetings' nor 'casual meetings' are synonyms for *invective*.

1.8(D)

---

3 Which sentence below best describes Kennedy's use of rhetorical devices in Sentence 19?

A   Kennedy used Logos to appeal to the audience's logical thoughts about modern warfare

B   Kennedy used Ethos to appeal to the audience's ethical thoughts about modern warfare

C   Kennedy used Ethos to appeal to the audience's belief in his credibility about modern warfare

D   Kennedy used Pathos to appeal to the audience's emotions about modern warfare

Answer D is correct. Kennedy used emotionally impacting phrases throughout this sentence, including *take comfort, overburdened, rightly alarmed,* and *balance of terror* within this sentence, appealing to the audience's emotions about the threat of war. **Answer C is a distractor.** Kennedy, the President of the United States, certainly had and used his credibility to convince the audience during this speech. However, in this sentence, he is appealing more to the audience's emotions about war then using his credibility about the subject of war. **Answers A and B are incorrect.** No true logical argument was made in this sentence, Kennedy did not provide any facts or statistics to back up his words. Answer B is incorrect simply on the basis of the mismatch between the answers rhetorical device (Ethos) and it's supporting words (ethical thoughts); these words would support more of a Pathos appeal than an Ethos appeal.

1.8(G)

4 This speech is an Argumentative Text characterized by all of the following except -

    F   it includes facts, and is not based on the speaker's opinions

    G   it has a thesis statement that is the focus of the speech

    H   it concludes with a call to action

    J   it begins with a claim followed by multiple clear, supporting details

Answer F is correct. This is a characteristic of informational text, not argumentative texts. While effective argumentative texts will use a lot of facts, these are used to back a speaker's opinion on the subject, not to simply present the facts as in informational texts. **Answers G, H and J are incorrect**. These are all characteristics of argumentative texts that are present in this speech.

1.7(E)

> "And so, my fellow Americans: ask not what your country can do for you--ask what you can do for your country."

5 What was Kennedy trying to convey to the audience with this statement?

    A   The audience should stop asking for handouts and start working for the government

    B   The audience should recommit to the national loyalty described in the speech

    C   The audience should prepare to defend freedom at its darkest hour

    D   The audience should work towards making the described goals a reality

Answer D is correct. Kennedy made a plea for the citizens of America to help him fulfill his goals, starting with Sentence 32 and ending with Sentence 42, the call to action 'ask not what your country…' In this call, he was requesting Americans to rise up, as they had in the past, to meet the new challenges to make mankind better. **Answer A is a distractor**. This answer goes slightly off topic – Kennedy never really addressed welfare programs within the United States, nor did he suggest that people must work *for* the government, rather, they should work *with* the government for the betterment of people. **Answers B and C are incorrect**. While there was certainly some national pride evident in this speech, Kennedy did not call for the audience to recommit to this pride. He also did mention that America would be prepared for war, but not to prepare Americans for defense, as he stated America would strive for peaceful resolutions first.

1.8(A)

---

6 Which of the following sentences best summarizes Kennedy's primary claim?

    F   America and its allies, when cooperating, will have amazing accomplishments and will defeat any challenge that presents itself

    G   Everyone should understand that America will meet any challenge to help our allies and defeat our foes to protect our nation's sovereignty and goals.

    H   America pledges to support and defend our new allies and, even if they disagree with some of our views, hope they will agree that freedom is better than tyranny

    J   Everyone should believe that America, as the primary superpower of the global community, will protect and defend our borders to safeguard our freedom

Answer G is correct. In his opening statement, Kennedy expresses to *every nation* regardless of their intents towards America (everyone), should know America will *pay any price*, *bear any burden*, *meet any hardship* (meet any challenge), *support any friend* (help our allies), *oppose any foe* (defeat our foes) to *assure the survival and success of liberty* (protect our nation's sovereignty and goals). **Answers F, H and J are incorrect**. All of these are facets of the evidence Kennedy provided on how the country will solve the problem of 'assuring the survival and success of liberty.'

1.7(E)(i)

7 What evidence does Kennedy provide to demonstrate he is committed to peace and cooperation among adversaries?

    A   He commits to a reduction in nuclear weapons to ensure peace between nations

    B   He challenges adversaries with America's strength to help prevent future violence

    C   He provides alternative paths to adversaries that would lead to a common good

    D   He assures all nations that he is taking steps to avoid conflicts in the world

Answer C is correct. Kennedy dedicates 12 sentences (Sentences 16 – 28) to this part of his message, a full 25% of his speech. Summarized, he requests peace, outlines America's strength, offers to negotiate and explore problems that unite them, including cooperation in the stars, with disease, etc. and to join together in strength to help preserve peace. **Answers B and D are distractors**. While Kennedy does subtlety describe America's strength as a deterrent to war and hence a way to peace, using this as the best demonstration of his commitment to peace and cooperation is an oversimplification. Similarly, Kennedy does not say he will avoid conflicts in the world, rather that adversaries should try, instead of building up new weapons of destruction, to build new endeavors and cooperation that would help mankind. **Answer A is incorrect**. Kennedy never implied that America would reduce nuclear weapons, only that America was committed to both sides formulating inspections and controls for these weapons.

E1.7(E)(ii)

---

8 Who was the intended audience of Kennedy's Inaugural Address?

    F   American citizens

    G   World citizens

    H   America and its free allies

    J   Communist nations around the world

Answer G is correct. Kennedy addresses the entire world in his introduction and speech (old and new allies, struggling nations, border nations, United Nations and adversaries). It is clear Kennedy intended for a global audience to hear his words and his commitment to the world. **Answers F and H are distractors**. Kennedy, as the United States President, was of course addressing American citizens as his primary audience, and includes America and its new and old free allies within the first 6 sentences. However, Kennedy goes on to address other worlds nations including struggling nations and adversaries. **Answer J is incorrect**. While Kennedy did spend a large amount of time addressing Communist nations (identified as adversaries), this is only a small part of his intended audience.

E1.7(E)(iii)

---

9 Which of the following logical fallacies could most likely be construed in Kennedy's speech?

    A   Straw man in Sentences 32 – 34

    B   Red Herring in Sentences 9 – 10

    C   Slippery Slope in Sentences 29 – 31

    D   Bandwagon in Sentences 35 – 37

Answer D is correct. In Sentence 35, Kennedy likens a call from a battle trumpet to a call to struggle against tyranny, poverty, disease and war. He then asks a rhetorical question of the North, South, East and West, providing the outcome of assuring "*a more fruitful life for all mankind*". Finally, he asks, "Will you join in that historic effort?", expecting a positive answer. This most closely represents a Bandwagon appeal. **Answer B is a distractor**. Sentence 10, especially, creates a False Dilemma (if you can't help the poor, you can't save the rich), but this is not a Red Herring. **Answers A and C are incorrect**. Kennedy did not use an oversimplification or attempt to refute any point in Sentences 32-34. Also, although Kennedy is expressing a timeline for how long his goals will take to reach fruition, he is not offering a counter to this that will occur if his path is not followed in Sentences 29-31.

E1.8(E)

1 Which of the following correctly describes the organizational pattern used in the Declaration of Independence passage?

A **Proposition and Support** - because it makes a statement at the beginning and provides the reasoning to support that statement throughout the passage

B **Compare and Contrast** – because it states what government should be and then contrasts this to the way government is under the king throughout the passage

C **Description** – because it describes what facets of government the colonists are not satisfied with and provides details about these facets throughout the passage

D **Chronological** – because it explains the status of the colonies and provides a chronology of the royal offenses to clarify how the colonies got to this state throughout the passage

Answer A is correct. The passage starts Sentence 2 (known as the Preamble) with a strong proposition, that *all men are created equal*, they have *certain unalienable rights*, including *Life, Liberty and the pursuit of happiness*, *governments are instituted* to secure these rights, and when *governments become destructive of these ends*, people can abolish them and *institute new government*(s) to best secure their rights. The passage then provides support for this statement, mostly how Great Britain was destructive and how the colonies thus are abolishing that government and instituting a new one, throughout the remainder of the passage. Finally, it ties back, albeit loosely, to the idea of *Life, Liberty*… with *our lives, our fortunes and our sacred honor*. **Answers B and C are distractors**. Although there was some compare and contrast between what an oppressive government is and what a good government should be, this was not the overall text structure used in this passage. Also, the descriptions of what areas of government the colonists were not satisfied with and details of these grievances were mentioned, but not as the organizational pattern for this reading. **Answer D is incorrect**. There is very little evidence that this passage was written in a chronological format.

E1.8(B)

2 What is the purpose of the capitalizations of words throughout the document within the sentences?

F This was done to establish the environment of the document

G This was done as a code to provide colonial insurgents with instructions

H This was done to show emphasis

J This was done as part of the writer's individual style

Answer H is correct. The capitalizations were done on a document that was hand written. Therefore, bold print to form emphasis would be very difficult. Instead, the document used capitalizations to show words within the passage that the authors felt were important. **Answers F, G and J are distractors**. The words do establish help establish the author's tone by stressing certain words, but not the environment. Also, there is no evidence that this was a code for insurgents; indeed, the Declaration of Independence is quite forward with the colonies' intent to break from England, and thus declare war. Finally, the writer's individual style is extremely evident within this document, but style aesthetics alone are not the reason the author capitalized these words.

E1.8(D)

> "We hold these Truths to be self-evident, that all Men are created equal"

3   This quote can best be referred to as –

A   an overstatement, because truths are not self-evident

B   an understatement, because all men are always created equal

C   an overstatement because truths are not self-evident and an understatement because all men are always created equal

D   neither an overstatement nor an understatement

Answer D is correct. Neither of these sentences are over- or understatements. Examples of how this quote could have been made into these types of statements would be **We hold all Truth to be self-evident** (overstatement – not ALL truth is self-evident, some truth must be researched and proven) and **that some men are created equal** (understatement – the original ALL is appropriate and reflects the truth that all men are created equally.) **Answers A, B and C are distractors**. These answers twist the words used by the author slightly to make them sound plausible, but they are all incorrect. Answer A stresses the word, *truths*, while removing the context (a limited 'these truths') to create an overstatement that does not exist. Answer B similarly uses the word 'always' to restate what the author has already said (there is no difference between 'all men' and 'all men always' in this restatement). This could lead the student to choose this answer when it is not correct. Answer C is simply a combination of both of these answers to provide yet another incorrect option that could, on the surface, seem correct.

E1.8(G)

4   Based on the passage, what can we infer was the author's primary purpose for writing the Declaration of Independence?

F   To initiate war with Britain and request foreign support

G   To prevent war with Britain and propose a new government

H   To declare war with Britain and denounce the king's actions

J   To justify war with Britain and establish an independent government

Answer J is correct. There are many clues to drive the student to this answer. In the first sentence, the author opens with *they should declare the causes which impel them to the separation*, providing the general purpose was to justify their actions. Sentence 21 provides the second part, by closing with the 'therefore' that established the independence and government of the *Independent States*. Given the choices provided, this answer is the most correct. **Answers F and H are distractors**. Although the document did indeed initiate war with Britain and had a secondary purpose of getting the colonies' story to foreign governments (with the hope of raising capital and support for the war), this answer lacks the establishment of the new colonial government, a key purpose of this writing. Likewise, although this document was akin to a declaration of war with Britain and it also denounced the king's actions *en masse*, the purpose of establishing the independent government is missing from Answer H. **Answer G is incorrect**. The "shot heard round the world" was never going to *prevent* war with Britain, making this answer incorrect from the outset. Even so, there are also no contextual clues or evidence in the writing that prevention of war was the desired outcome.

E1.8(A)

5 Which of the following sentences best describes the author's primary claims?

A   When certain unacceptable events in life take place, man must rise up against his oppressors to take back their rights and protect their freedom

B   The king has betrayed his colonies by causing or allowing offenses to be perpetuated on the colonists and thus his rule of law is no longer valid

C   People are all made equally and they own certain rights and have a duty to defend their rights, the rights of others and even replace governments when these rights are denied

D   Rebellion is the just and noble duty of all citizens of free nations when met with oppression from outside forces and all men have a duty to protect themselves from oppressors

Answer C is correct. This is a very simplified version of Sentences 2 – 5 (all men are equal, have rights, government either supports these rights or is replaced, etc.), where the author's primary claims are found. **Answers A, B and D are distractors**. None of these answers provide as complete a synopsis as Answer C. Answer A includes the claim of rising up against oppressive governments to protect man's freedom, but ignores the remainder. Answer B stresses the 'oppressive' portion of the claims and provides for the separation from England, but is missing the equality and rights. Answer D also includes only the rising up and protecting of rights and excludes the other claims.

E1.7(E)(i)

> "The History of the present King of Great-Britain is a History of repeated Injuries and Usurpations, all having in direct Object the Establishment of an absolute Tyranny over these States."

6 What evidence does the writer present in the passage to support the opinion articulated in this quotation?

F   A statement explaining the *long Train of Abuses and Usurpations* and how these have impacted the colonies

G   A list of issues

H   A statement explaining that the colony must *acquiesce in the necessity, which denounces our Separation*

J   A list of responsibilities

Answer G is correct. The passage provided 5 of the 27 grievances (issues) that all support the quotation. **Answers F and H are distractors**. These answers use words from the text, out of context, but these were not directly supporting the quotation within the passage. **Answer J is incorrect**. Government being responsible for the upholding and protection of rights was discussed, but a list of responsibilities was not provided.

E1.7(E)(ii)

---

7 Who is the intended audience of this passage?

A   The world

B   The colonies

C   The King of Great Britain

D   Foreign allies and supporters

Answer A is correct. The crafters of the Declaration of Independence intended their message to be shown to the world. Evidence for this comes from Sentence 1 (*respect to the opinions of mankind*) and Sentence 7 (*submitted to a candid world*). **Answers B, C and D are distractors**. Individually, each of these (colonies, king and foreign allies) are all part of the intended audience, but as only portions of the intended whole, these are not the best answers.

E1.7(E)(iii)

8 The conclusion of the Declaration of Independence was –

F   effective because it restated the main ideas and supporting evidence in a new way

G   ineffective because it failed to restate the main ideas and supporting evidence in a new way

H   effective because it provided a resolution and resulting actions as expected based on the passage's organizational pattern

J   ineffective because it failed to provide a resolution and resulting actions as expected based on the passage's organizational pattern

Answer H is correct. This conclusion was effective because it closed the proposition and support organizational pattern with a course of action that logically follows as a result of the proposition. **Answer F, G and J are incorrect**. This essay did not restate main idea and supporting evidence as an expository essay would, but this was because of the organizational pattern used, not because it was ineffective. Answer J is incorrect because it did provide a resolution and resulting actions as appropriate for this text structure.

E1.7(E)(i)

Connections Across Genres: Questions Part 1

1 All of the following statements differ between "If…" (page 71) and "Annabel Lee" (page 77) except –

A   the overall mood and tone of the poem

B   the consistency of the poetic structure

C   the narrator's dedication towards his subject

D   the message intended for the reader

Answer C is correct. In both texts, the narrator's dedication towards their subjects is evident. In "Annabel Lee", this dedication takes the form of obsession while in "If…", the dedication takes the form of fatherly advice. **Answer D is a distractor**. While the dedication of the narrators might be similar, this does not hold true for the message intended for the reader. In "If…", the reader can take away the message of hopefulness for the future despite dealing with the hardships that come with life. In "Annabel Lee", the message is a dark version of 'Love never dies'. **Answers A and B are incorrect**. Both the mood and tone as well as the poetic consistency of these texts differ significantly.

E1.4(E)

2 In the "Inaugural Address of John F. Kennedy" (page 145), what global crisis can you infer most likely inspired his speech?

F   World War II

G   The Nuclear Arms Race

H   The Civil War

J   The American Revolution

Answer G is correct. No understanding or knowledge of historical events is required to answer this question. There are several contextual clues within the passage to lead the student to this conclusion. Line 16's "before the dark powers of destruction…", Line 18's "For only when our arms are sufficient…" and Line 19's "steady spread of the deadly atom, yet both racing to alter that uncertain balance of terror…" are key to this answer. **Answer F is a distractor**. Given all the 'world' talk within this text, if close reading is not utilized, the student might choose this answer. World War II, however, is many years past by the time of this speech and is not relevant. **Answers H and J are incorrect**. Nothing within the passage would lead the student to believe it was inspired by either of these events and no references to either event exist in the speech.

E1.4(E)

3 After reading the "Inaugural Address of John F. Kennedy" (page 145) and *Frankenstein* (page 53), what can be understood about human nature?

  A   The inventions of mankind can become horrible

  B   Mankind is driven towards war

  C   Science and technological advancements of mankind are inherently evil

  D   Man should not perform genetic experimentation on humans

Answer A is correct. Based on the passages, we can infer that both authors would agree with this statement. Kennedy in Line 19 used words like, "deadly", "terror" and "final war" to describe nuclear weapons, while Shelley in Lines 24 – 25 used "horror" and "hideous" when describing Frankenstein's creation, the monster. **Answer C is a distractor**. Although scientific and technological advances can be used for evil purposes, they are not inherently evil. As Kennedy suggested in Lines 25 – 26, science can be used to improve life. **Answers B and D are incorrect**. Neither text suggested mankind is driven towards war, and although *Frankenstein* does imply that the experimentation with the human form was a mistake, Kennedy does not mention this similarly in his speech.

E1.4(H)

4 What literary element is similar between *A Christmas Carol* (page 45) and "Annabel Lee" (page 77)?

  F   A heavy use of dialogue to characterize the protagonist

  G   An extended metaphor that represents the author

  H   A strong narrative voice that critiques the protagonist's actions

  J   Sensory details that contribute to a dark and foreboding mood

Answer J is correct. In both passages, an overall dark and foreboding mood is established by the authors. In *A Christmas Carol*, this comes in the form of the characterization of the Phantom and how it affected Scrooge. In "Annabel Lee", the author uses the general feeling of loss within the narrator's life and his dark obsession with his dead Annabel. **Answer H is a distractor**. This narrative voice exists in *A Christmas Carol* with respect to Scrooge, but not in "Annabel Lee" **Answers F and G are incorrect**. Neither passage relies on a heavy use of dialogue, indeed there is none at all in "Annabel Lee." Also, no information was given that the author is being represented within either passage, so the student should have no reason to choose Answer G (even given the life of the narrator in "Annabel Lee" was, in fact, loosely based on Poe's life, this is not the case with *A Christmas Carol*.)

E1.6

5 What lesson can be learned from reading "The Declaration of Independence" (page 155)?

  A   Government should be providing rights for its people

  B   You are responsible for defending your natural rights

  C   Problems should be solved through warfare

  D   Happiness is determined through the government's effectiveness

Answer B is correct. Among the themes of the natural rights of equality, life, liberty and the pursuit of happiness is the duty one has to protect and defend these rights, even from their own government. **Answer A is a distractor**. The text states that Government is responsible for securing the rights, not providing them. **Answers C and D are incorrect**. The text stated that this course (leading to overthrow of the government and warfare) should not be taken lightly. Also, nowhere in the text is happiness shown to be determined by government effectiveness, only that man can pursue happiness as a right.

E1.4(E)

6 All of the following are differences between Informational and Argumentative texts except –

F the use of research, facts and evidence

G the purpose of the text is to support an author's claim

H the text is structured and concise with an easy-to-read layout

J the importance of rhetoric in conveying the message

Answer F is correct. Both Informational and Argumentative rely on, at their core, research, facts and evidence. Without these, there is little difference between these genres and Fictional works. **Answers G, H and J are incorrect**. Answers G and J are characteristics of Argumentative texts while Answer H is an example of Informational text.

E1.7

---

7 We can infer from "The Inaugural Address of John F. Kennedy" (page 145) and *Romeo and Juliet* (page 93) the importance of –

A Tenacity

B War

C Peace

D Strength

Answer C is correct. Kennedy stresses the importance of peace between nations and even urges his adversaries to "begin anew the quest for peace." Similarly, Romeo implores Tybalt to cease fighting before Mercutio is tragically killed. **Answer D is a distractor**. Though strength is an important quality to have in these situations, as is implied in *Romeo and Juliet* by the fighting prowess of both combatants and stated by Kennedy in his speech, the importance of avoiding violence and the emphasis on peaceful resolutions are more evident, especially given the outcome of the fight in *Romeo and Juliet*. **Answers A and B are incorrect**. Tenacity and War may be concepts in these passages, but they are not the main focus.

E1.8

---

8 What is a similar motif between both *A Brief History of NASA* (page 129) and *Frankenstein* (page 53)?

F Historical events

G Loss

H World development

J Technological advancements

Answer J is correct. *A Brief History of NASA* highlights a timeline of NASA's advancements in the realm of space exploration. *Frankenstein* tells the story of a scientist and his monstrous creation, arguably an advancement in the study of medicine or anatomy; both of these provide examples of technological advancement. **Answer H is a distractor**. Neither NASA (as America's space program) or Frankenstein (as a creator of a humanoid creature) provide the scale of impact to consider them 'World development.' Even should one argue for NASA in this case, there would be little case for the monster, so at best this answer is only half correct. **Answer F and G are incorrect**. *Frankenstein* does mention loss vaguely in the form of a premonition, and the timeline covers historical events, but these are not similar for both of them.

E1.4(E)

1 All of the following similarities exists between the protagonists of *Frankenstein* (page 53) and *A Christmas Carol* (page 45) except –

A   they both experience terror

B   they both have a sense of disappointment in themselves

C   they both have to learn a difficult lesson

D   they both hide from their fears

Answer D is correct. Although Doctor Frankenstein does run away from his monster to hide, Scrooge engages with his ghosts as he knows it will do him good, as mentioned in Line 44. **Answers A, B and C are incorrect.** Both of the protagonists experience terror at the eerie, supernatural figures they encounter (or created). Both protagonists have also made mistakes in their lives that are disappointments, as Scrooge implies in Line 44 and Frankenstein implies in many lines, most notably Lines 13 and 18. Scrooge's difficult lesson is fairly direct within the text, causing him to 'lose his legs' in Line 39, while Frankenstein's difficult lesson is more subtle, hinted at by his dream premonition and his fearful encounters with his own creation.

E1.4(E)

2 The murder of Mercutio in *Romeo and Juliet* (page 93) could spark what modern debate?

F   The right to bear arms

G   The right to defend yourself

H   The right of due process

J   The freedom of expression

Answer F is correct. If this occurred in modern times, Mercutio's very public and violent death amidst many characters bearing arms (swords) could spark this debate, especially given the highborn nature of the victim. **Answer G is a distractor**. Self-defense as a right is an argument in a debate for the right to bear arms, rather than a hot-button modern debate topic on its own. Even if the student considers this as a plausible answer, the right to bear arms should be considered the superior choice. **Answers H and J are incorrect.** Neither of these topics are relevant in this scene as no judgement was handed down, arbitrarily or otherwise, to bring about Mercutio's murder, and although both combatants did express themselves (negatively towards the other), neither was forbidden from doing so, nor did this bring about Mercutio's murder.

E1.4(E)

3 What purpose does the organizational pattern of *A Brief History of NASA* (page 129) and *The Pirates' Who's Who* (page 121) serve?

A   To inform the reader on the lives of individuals within the passages

B   To inform the reader on a series of sequential events

C   To inform the reader on a series of unrelated events

D   To inform the reader on the technologies developed within the passages

Answer B is correct. Both of the passages are organized in chronological order of events to provide information on a sequence of events. **Answer C is a distractor**. The events in both passages follow related events that characterize the timelines of both subjects. **Answers A and D are incorrect**. Pirate Roberts' life is characterized, but NASA was focused on the space program and not on individuals. Furthermore, NASA's timeline does highlight technology, but no technology is mentioned within the passage from *The Pirates' Who's Who*.

E1.4(H)

4 What literary element is present in both *The Pirates' Who's Who* (page 121) and *Romeo and Juliet* (page 93)?

    F Both use similes to represent the death of a character

    G Both use metaphors to represent the death of a character

    H Both have a character who is hot-headed and violent

    J Both have a character who is benevolent and tries to seek peace

Answer H is correct. Both Pirate Roberts and Tybalt are savage and short-tempered characters, one razing a fort, bombarding a town and setting fire to ships in an act of revenge and the other killing a man under the arm of another man who is restraining his opponent from fighting. **Answers F and G are distractors.** Though both passages mention the death of a character, there are no metaphors or similes to represent this concept. **Answer J is incorrect.** Romeo does try to seek peace, but no such character is found in *The Pirates' Who's Who.*

E1.6

---

5 What do you predict will happen to the relationship between Diana and Enid in *He Said, She Said* (page 103), based on the reading passage?

    A The relationship between Diana and Enid will be strained

    B The relationship between Diana and Enid will be enhanced

    C The relationship between Diana and Enid will be ended

    D The relationship between Diana and Enid will remain the same

Answer A is correct. Due to their bickering in the script, it can be inferred that Diana and Enid will have a very awkward and strained relationship moving forward. **Answer C is a distractor.** It is evident that the women, though strained, still have some thread of friendship as implied in Line 29 when Enid stops Diana from leaving in anger. **Answer B and D are incorrect.** There is little evidence to support Diana and Enid's relationship remaining the same or becoming better (enhanced) within this passage.

E1.4(E)

---

6 All of the following are differences between Poetry and Fiction texts except –

    F the use of text features that form the shape of the text on the page

    G the use of sensory details and vivid language

    H the description always includes imaginary events, people and / or places

    J the use of rhythm and / or rhyme within the text

Answer G is correct. Poetry and Fiction both feature vivid details to communicate the author's message effectively to the reader. **Answer H is a distractor.** Fictional works <u>always</u> have some imaginary elements (else they would be Nonfictional like Informational texts), but this is not always the case in poetry. Poetry can describe <u>real or imaginary</u> events, people and / or places. **Answers F and J are incorrect.** Text features, like forming shapes with words, and rhymes characterize poetry, not fiction.

E1.7

7 The authors attempt to _____ in the subject of both "If..." (page 71) and *A Christmas Carol* (page 45)?

A   inspire motivation

B   inspire change

C   inspire improvement

D   inspire fear

Answer C is correct. Both authors are attempting to inspire improvement in the subjects: "If..." contains fatherly advice prompting this change through encouragement and motivation, while in *A Christmas Carol* the author highlights the supernatural and ghost encounters to guide the improvement of Scrooge. **Answer B is a distractor**. While this answer is correct, the authors are attempting to inspire change *for the better*, not simply change. As the word 'improvement' is superior to the word 'change' when conveying this meaning, this is not the best answer. **Answers A and D are incorrect.** "If..." is a motivational poem, however, while Scrooge is being motivated to change, this is driven by a supernatural event, and the ghosts are not trying to inspire him to be motivated. Also, while "If..." does warn about some of the trials in life, this is not done to inspire fear, and indeed, although there are some fearful moments in the passage from *A Christmas Carol*, the author's theme was not fear, but the goodness of changing for the better.

E1.8

This page intentionally left blank.

Teacher Support Pages

Teachers,

The following sections are provided to enhance your experience with this workbook and to make it easier to incorporate it into your plan of instruction. It was our pleasure to provide you with this English I teaching aid, and we hope you enjoy using it in your classroom.

The support pages include:

At a glance: Section Content with Page Numbers

At a glance: Vocabulary / Concepts in each Section

At a glance: TEKS Applied in each Section

Assessment Record Pages

If you would like any of these in a printable, PDF format, please email us at:

Support@TheAngrySchnauzer.com

Please include in the subject line: **STAAR English I Teacher**

Thank you!

The Angry Schnauzer

The Angry Schnauzer

Section Content (with Page Numbers)

	Writing Section: Editing Lesson (Pages 1 - 16)	Writing Section: Revision Lesson (Pages 19 - 37)	Fiction Section (Pages 39 - 64)	Poetry Section (Pages 65 - 86)	Drama Section (Pages 87 - 114)	Informational Texts Section (Pages 115 - 138)	Argumentative Texts Section (Pages 139 - 166)	Connections Across Genres (Pages 167 - 188)
Targeted Terminology	pages 3 - 6	page 21	pages 41 - 42	pages 67 - 68	page 89	pages 117 - 118	pages 141 - 142	pages 169 - 170
Painless Practice	pages 7 - 8	page 23	page 43	page 69	page 91	pages 119 - 120	page 143	page 171
Read & Review Questions Part 1	pages 9 - 12	pages 25 - 28	pages 45 - 50	pages 71 - 74	pages 93 - 100	pages 121 - 125	pages 145 - 151	pages 173 - 175
Read & Review Questions Part 2	pages 13 - 16	pages 29 - 32	pages 53 - 57	pages 77 - 80	pages 103 - 108	pages 129 - 131	pages 155 - 160	pages 179 - 181
Essay Skills		pages 35 - 37	pages 61 - 64	pages 83 - 86	pages 111 - 114	pages 135 - 138	pages 163 - 166	pages 185 - 188
Read & Review Answers Part 1	pages 191 - 193	pages 195 - 198	pages 201 - 204	pages 207 - 208	pages 211 - 213	pages 215 - 217	pages 220 - 222	pages 226 - 228
Read & Review Answers Part 2	pages 193 - 195	pages 198 - 201	pages 204 - 206	pages 209 - 210	pages 213 - 215	pages 218 - 219	pages 223 - 226	pages 229 - 231

This page intentionally left blank.

Vocabulary / Concepts Covered within each Section

Writing: Editing Lesson:

- Editing
- Conventions
- Craft / Style
- Publish
- Noun
- Pronoun
- Verb
- Adverb
- Adjective
- Punctuation
- Syntax
- Complete Sentence
- Independent Clause
- Dependent Clause (Sentence Fragment)

- Noun Clause
- Adjective Clause
- Adverb Clause
- Structure
- Simple Sentence
- Compound Sentence
- Complex Sentence
- Compound-Complex Sentence
- Conjunction
- Coordinating Conjunction
- Correlative Conjunction

- Subordinating Conjunction
- Active Voice
- Passive Voice
- Run-on Sentence
- Comma Splice
- Fused Sentence
- Subject-Verb-Pronoun Agreement
- Verb Tense Consistency
- Noun-Pronoun (Pronoun Antecedent) Agreement

Writing: Revision Lesson:

- Revision
- Correspondence
- Controlling Idea
- Clarity
- Diction
- Style

- Coherence
- Development
- Organization
- Friendly Structure
- Professional Structure

- Parallel Construction
- Point of View
- Annotate
- Paraphrase
- Commentary

Fiction Section:

- Fiction
- Author's Purpose
- Theme
- Setting
- Plot
- Linear Plot
- Non-linear Plot
- Unresolved
- Flashback
- Foreshadow
- Parallel plot

- Subplot
- Mood
- Tone
- Characterization
- Character foil
- Conflict
- Narrator
- 1st Person Narrator
- 2nd Person Narrator
- 3rd Person-limited Narrator

- 3rd Person-omniscient Narrator
- Figurative language
- Irony – Literary
- Dramatic Irony
- Situational Irony
- Verbal Irony
- Compare
- Contrast

Poetry Section:

- Poetry
- Audience
- Message
- Line
- Explicit
- Implicit
- Overstatement
- Understatement
- Stanza
- Couplet
- Tercet
- Quatrain
- Rhyme Scheme
- Voice
- Diction
- Prosody
- Oxymoron
- Analogy
- Alliteration
- Assonance
- Consonance

Drama Section:

- Drama
- Playwright
- Act
- Scene
- Stage directions
- Dialogue
- Monologue
- Soliloquies
- Asides
- Parody
- Satire

Informational Text Section:

- Informational Text
- Graphic Feature
- Print Feature
- Text Structure (Organizational Pattern)
- Sequence and Order
- Cause and Effect
- Problem and Solution
- Compare and Contrast
- Description
- Proposition and Support
- Thesis
- Details
- Evidence
- Opinion
- Contradictory
- Explanatory Essay
- Personal Essay
- Reports
- Summary

Argumentative Text Section:

- Argument
- Message
- Claim
- Refute
- Counterargument (Rebuttal)
- Concession
- Rhetorical Devices
- Ethos
- Pathos
- Logos
- Significant
- Sensory Images
- Current Events
- Eyewitnesses
- Overestimate
- Underestimate
- Logical Fallacies
- Red Herring
- Strawman
- Slippery Slope
- Bandwagon
- Either-Or (False Dilemma)
- Begging the Question

Connections Across Genres Section:

- Text-to-Text
- Text-to-Self
- Text-to-World

TEKS Applied (by Section)

Writing Section: Editing Lesson

TEKS Applied	Short Title	Location(s)
E1.9(D)(i)	Complete, controlled sentences	– Part 1, Question 1
E1.9(D)(i)	Run-on sentences	– Part 1, Question 2
E1.9(D)(i)	Sentence splices	– Part 1, Question 9
E1.9(D)(i)	Fragments	– Part 2, Question 1
E1.9(D)(ii)	Active / Passive Voice	– Part 2, Question 2
E1.9(D)(ii)	Verb tense	– Part 1, Question 3; – Part 2, Question 8
E1.9(D)(iii)	Pronoun-antecedent agreement	– Part 1, Question 4; – Part 2, Question 6
E1.9(D)(iv)	Correct capitalization	– Part 1, Question 5; – Part 2, Question 5
E1.9(D)(v)	Commas	– Part 1, Question 6
E1.9(D)(v)	Colons	– Part 1, Question 7
E1.9(D)(v)	Semicolons	– Part 2, Question 4
E1.9(D)(v)	Quotations	– Part 2, Question 7
E1.9(D)(vi)	Spelling	– Part 1, Question 8; – Part 2, Question 3

Writing Section: Revision Lesson

TEKS Applied	Short Title	Location(s)
E1.9(C)	Clarity	– Part 1, Question 1; – Part 2, Question 8
E1.9(C)	Development	– Part 1, Question 2; – Part 2, Question 9
E1.9(C)	Organization	– Part 1, Question 3; – Part 2, Question 7
E1.9(C)	Style	– Part 1, Question 4; – Part 2, Question 6
E1.9(C)	Diction	– Part 1, Question 5; – Part 2, Question 5
E1.9(C)	Placement of phrases	– Part 1, Question 6; – Part 2, Question 2
E1.9(C)	Parallel constructions	– Part 1, Question 7; – Part 2, Question 3
E1.9(C)	Dependent clauses	– Part 1, Question 8; – Part 2, Question 1
E1.9(C)	Main idea	– Part 1, Question 9; – Part 2, Question 4

Fiction Section

TEKS Applied	Short Title	Location(s)
E1.2	Vocabulary	– Part 1, Question 7
E1.2(B)	Analyze context to find meaning	– Part 1, Question 6
E1.4	Comprehension	– Part 1, Question 8
E1.4(F)	Inferences using evidence	– Part 2, Question 8
E1.6	Literary elements	– Part 2, Question 6
E1.6(B)	Characterization	– Part 1, Question 1
E1.6(D)	Setting	– Part 1, Question 2; – Part 2, Question 3
E1.7	Genre	– Part 2, Question 7
E1.8(A)	Author's purpose	– Part 2, Question 1
E1.8(D)	Use of language	– Part 1, Question 3; – Part 1, Question 9 – Part 2, Question 2
E1.8(E)	Irony	– Part 1, Question 4
E1.8(F)	Tone	– Part 1, Question 5
E1.8(F)	Mood	– Part 2, Question 4
E1.8(G)	Overstatements	– Part 2, Question 5

Poetry Section

TEKS Applied	Short Title	Location(s)
E1.2(A)	Dictionary use	– Part 2, Question 3
E1.2(B)	Analyze context	– Part 2, Question 4
E1.4(D)	Interpret mental images	– Part 1, Question 6
E1.4(E)	Making connections	– Part 1, Question 5
E1.4(F)	Make inferences using evidence	– Part 2, Question 6
E1.7(B)	Alliteration (or Anaphora)	– Part 1, Question 2
E1.8	Author's craft	– Part 1, Question 4
E1.8(A)	Message	– Part 2, Question 5
E1.8(D)	Use of language	– Part 2, Question 1
E1.8(E)	Personification	– Part 1, Question 3
E1.8(F)	Tone	– Part 1, Question 1
E1.8(F)	Diction	– Part 2, Question 2

Drama Section

TEKS Applied	Short Title	Location(s)
E1.2(B)	Analyze context	– Part 1, Question 7
E1.2(C)	Meaning of foreign words	– Part 1, Question 8
E1.6	Literary elements	– Part 2, Question 6
E1.6(A)	Analyze theme through characterization	– Part 1, Question 2; – Part 2, Question 1
E1.6(B)	Character foils	– Part 1, Question 3
E1.6(B)	Characterization	– Part 2, Question 2
E1.6(D)	Setting influence on theme	– Part 2, Question 3
E1.7	Genre	– Part 2, Question 5
E1.7(A)	Read & respond to British Literature	– Part 1, Question 1
E1.7(C)	Dramatic conventions	– Part 1, Question 4; – Part 2, Question 4
E1.8(D)	Use of language	– Part 1, Question 5
E1.8(E)	Literary devices	– Part 1, Question 6

Informational Texts Section

TEKS Applied	Short Title	Location(s)
E1.8(B)	Text structure	– Part 1, Question 1
E1.8(D)	Use of language	– Part 1, Question 2
E1.7(D)	Characteristics of genre	– Part 1, Question 3
E1.8	Author's purpose	– Part 1, Question 4
E1.8	Point of view	– Part 1, Question 5
E1.7(D)(i)	Thesis	– Part 1, Question 6
E1.7(D)(i)	Supporting evidence	– Part 1, Question 7
E1.7(D)(i)	Conclusion	– Part 1, Question 8
E1.7(D)	Structural elements	– Part 2, Question 1
E1.8(A)	Author's message	– Part 2, Question 2
E1.7(D)(ii)	Organizational structure to develop theme	– Part 2, Question 3
E1.8(C)	Use of print features	– Part 2, Question 4
E1.8(C)	Use of graphic features	– Part 2, Question 5
E1.4	Comprehension	– Part 2, Question 6

Argumentative Texts Section

TEKS Applied	Short Title	Location(s)
E1.7(E)	Characteristics of genre	– Part 1, Question 4
E1.7(E)(i)	Clear, arguable claim	– Part 1, Question 6; – Part 2, Question 5
E1.7(E)(i)	Conclusion	– Part 2, Question 8
E1.7(E)(ii)	Various types of evidence	– Part 1, Question 7; – Part 2, Question 6
E1.7(E)(iii)	Identifiable audience	– Part 1, Question 8; – Part 2, Question 7
E1.8(A)	Author's message	– Part 1, Question 5
E1.8(A)	Author's purpose	– Part 2, Question 4
E1.8(B)	Text structure	– Part 1, Question 1; – Part 2, Question 1
E1.8(D)	Use of language	– Part 1, Question 2; – Part 2, Question 2
E1.8(E)	Logical fallacies	– Part 1, Question 9
E1.8(G)	Rhetorical devices	– Part 1, Question 3; – Part 2, Question 3

Connections Across Genres Section

TEKS Applied	Short Title	Location(s)
E1.4(E)	Text-to-Text within genres	– Part 1, Question 1; – Part 2, Question 1
E1.4(E)	Text-to-World	– Part 1, Question 2; – Part 2, Question 2
E1.4(H)	Synthesize two texts	– Part 1, Question 3; – Part 2, Question 3
E1.6	Literary elements of multiple Texts	– Part 1, Question 4; – Part 2, Question 4
E1.4(E)	Text-to-Self	– Part 1, Question 5; – Part 2, Question 5
E1.7	Multiple genres	– Part 1, Question 6; – Part 2, Question 6
E1.8	Author's purpose across genres	– Part 1, Question 7; – Part 2, Question 7
E1.4(E)	Text-to-Text across genres	– Part 1, Question 8

ASSESSMENT RECORD

Assignment

Student Names

ASSESSMENT RECORD

Assignment

Student Names

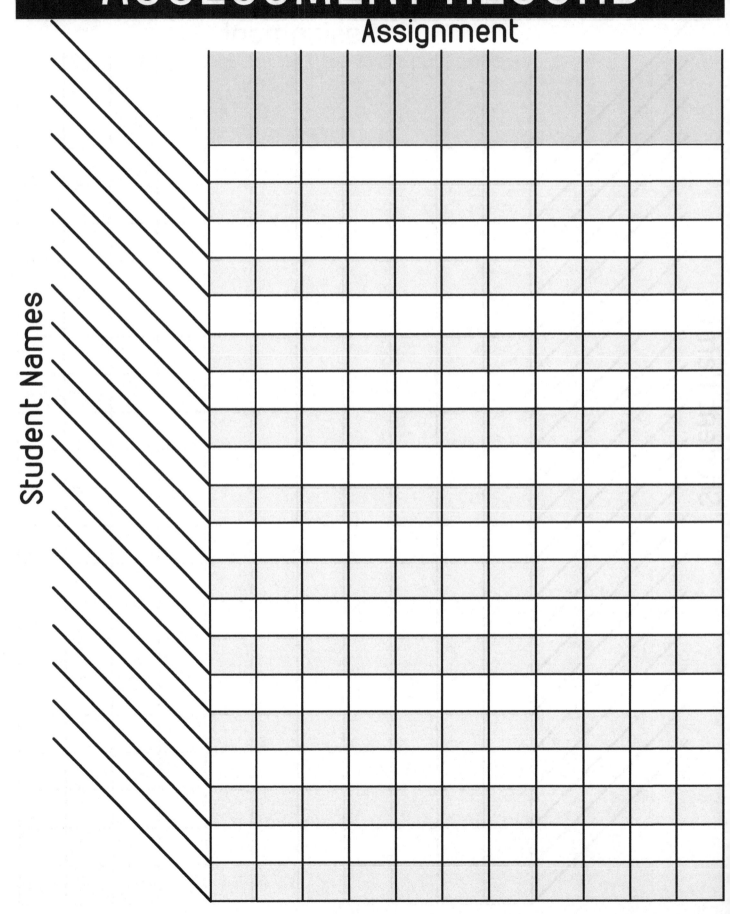

82508392R00138